ENTREPRENEURSHIP

Personal Development in Entrepreneurship

KING ARI DANE

ABOUT THE BOOK

You might wonder, why you picked up this book. Perhaps you know you want to be an entrepreneur and take charge of your own life. You've already got a great idea for a business you're sure will be a hit. Or perhaps you think, somewhere in the back of your mind, that maybe you might like to start your own business but you're not sure what venture to start, what entrepreneurship is like, and whether it's for you... Whichever of these categories you fall into, you are in the right place.

This book is designed as an integrated toolbox for first-time and repeat entrepreneurs so that they can build great enterprises based on innovative product and approach. Serial entrepreneurs with deep experience in a particular field or industry will also find these guides useful to more efficiently bring products to market.

It covers all you need to know about entrepreneurship ranging from the
Guides to succeeding at entrepreneurship,
Establishing a successful business by planning
Knowing your target market,
Financing
Entrepreneurer's attitude and so on

As they say, "there's no time like the present," so grab a cup of coffee, get comfortable, and let's start creating your business!

Entrepreneurship is a wild ride, but it's well worth buying a ticket as long as you're prepared for the highs and lows

So let's start

Legal & Disclaimer
The information contained in this book is focused on business, entrepreneurship and market inclined topics.
The content and information contained in this book has been compiled from sources deemed reliable, and it is accurate to the best of the Author's knowledge, information and belief. However, the Author cannot guarantee its accuracy and validity and cannot be held liable for any errors and/or omissions. It is sold with the understanding that the publisher is not engaged in rendering legal, accounting, or other professional services. If legal advice or other expert assistance is required, the services of a competent professional person should be sought.
Upon using the contents and information contained in this book, you agree to hold harmless the Author from and against any damages, costs, and expenses, including any legal fees potentially resulting from the application of any of the information provided by this book.
This disclaimer applies to any loss or damages caused by the use and application, whether directly or indirectly, of any advice or information presented, whether for breach of contract, tort, negligence, personal injury, criminal intent, or under any other cause of action.
You agree to accept all risks of using the information presented inside this book.

TABLE OF CONTENTS

INTRODUCTION

Personal development is an ongoing and life-long process during which everyone can improve their life quality by discovering themselves, developing their own talents and potential, increasing the chances of achieving important goals and dreams. Basically, by concentrating on our own personal development by setting specific goals in this direction, we are getting closer to improving our lives, which is very important in the world of entrepreneurship.

Personal development goals are set very individually. They differ from person to person and require a specific approach while defining them. Personal development includes many activities and here I will take you through the journey which can help YOU work better on their startups.

To be an entrepreneur is to think differently. While most people seek refuge, entrepreneurs take risks. They don't want a job; they want to create jobs. Their goal isn't to think outside the box as much as it is to own the box. Entrepreneurs don't follow the market; they define the market. This is the bold way of thinking like an entrepreneur.

Feel free to jump around based on your interests or read the book from beginning to end. Whether you are thinking of starting a business, celebrating your first year in business, or approaching ten years in business, you'll find tremendous value in reading this book.

The Guide To Succeeding At Entrepreneurship

When you have zero experience, zero credentials, and zero skills, it's tempting not to try. Your head fills with a million and one reasons why you should stay where you are -- focused on what you know.

The trouble is the voice in your head that wants to try anyway. You've always wanted to start a business, but you don't know how. You have a bucket list of ideas, but they feel out of reach. You want to get into shape, but your past says you can't.

Here's the truth: You can be a complete beginner and still win big.

Sometimes knowing nothing is an advantage because it inspires you to approach everything with an open mind. When you challenge yourself to grow through action, odds are you'll find a way that works. Achieve something you didn't believe possible, and you'll destroy the artificial limits you've placed on yourself. Best of all, it's not as hard as you think. Here are five essentials that will help you achieve anything, even if you're starting from scratch.

1. Don't judge your starting point.

Compare yourself with people miles ahead of you, and you'll always feel inadequate. Everyone starts somewhere. It's much better to assess your progress by how far you've come rather than how far you need to go. All growth happens outside your comfort zone. If you try only the things you're confident you can do, you'll never realize how incredibly talented and resourceful you are.

2. Commit to consistent action.

Passion fuels the start of any new project. When that initial excitement evaporates, fear of mistakes, inevitable roadblocks and self-doubt creep in to hold you back. Counter these challenges by committing to consistent action.

You must fall in love with the work, not the result. Although sprints of work can accomplish goals, they don't create ongoing momentum. It's much more effective to set up systems and processes that force you to implement your plan of action daily. That way you can leverage the compound interest on continuous improvement. The same method works for any venture. Want to get better at cold-calling? Commit to five calls every day. Want to become more flexible? Stretch daily. Want to start a business? Set aside time to work on it every day. Time will give you everything you want, but you must be willing to commit to the long game.

3. Focus on being better tomorrow than you are today.

There's no such thing as an overnight success. Big accomplishments result from intentional action. You can't rush or shortcut the project. Growth is gradual, building on itself. Focus on 1 per cent improvement every day, and a visible transformation will develop over time. You'll refine your approach and get more efficient until a 1 per cent improvement is roughly equal to the improvement you experienced over the entire previous week. What's more, because you've built a habit, growth doesn't stop. A daily reflection was key to maintaining my consistency.

4. Fail as fast as you can.

If you don't know what you're doing, you'll inevitably get some things wrong. You've simply got to change your mindset around failure. People generally aren't scared to fail. They're afraid others will see them do it. Making mistakes is a huge part of growing and learning. Getting it wrong never feels good, but you can grab on to the opportunity to learn. You'll grow more quickly because you'll start making better mistakes. The faster you fall, the quicker you rise.

Relish the roadblocks and challenges. Be ready for things to get in your way when you're walking the harder path, and expect yourself to get through it. Success follows when you fight perfectionism with action in the spirit of learning, growing and becoming the best version of yourself.

In "Principles: Life and Work," hedge-fund founder and bestselling author Ray Dalio offers a compelling vision of that mindset: "It seems to me that if you look back on yourself a year ago and aren't shocked by how stupid you were, you haven't learned much."

5. Learn from people who've done what you want to do.

In today's world, you never have to start anything from scratch. Information is abundant out there. You don't have to go through anything with your eyes closed. Find people who are where you want to be, and follow their footsteps. Invest in mentors, courses, books, events, seminars, and workshops

Bonus tip: The sooner you start, the sooner you benefit.

The best time to start anything worth doing was 20 years ago. And the second-best time? It's right now. It doesn't matter if you have zero experience. All that matters is you're willing to learn, make mistakes and put in the work needed to actualize whatever it is you want to start. Just take another step, even if it's into the dark knowing you can figure it out. I can't wait to see what you start with the numerous ideas and skills garnered from the rest of the book.

SECTION ONE
STARTING YOUR BUSINESS

Discovery consists of seeing what everybody else has seen and thinking what nobody else has thought. - Albert von Szent-Györgyi

This section is designed as a road map to help you plan a course for your journey to business ownership. I am here to show you the best routes to take, help you avoid the potholes and road closures, and besides, navigate the curves and detours.

When you have zero experience, zero credentials, and zero skills, it's tempting not to try. Your head fills with a million and one reasons why you should stay where you are focused on what you know. The trouble is the voice in your head that wants to try anyway. You've always wanted to start a business, but you didn't know how. You have a bucket list of ideas, but they feel out of reach. You want to get into shape, but your past says you can't.

The truth is you can be a complete beginner and **Still Win Big.**

Sometimes knowing nothing is an advantage because it inspires you to approach everything with an open mind. When you challenge yourself to grow through action, odds are you'll find a way that works.

Starting your business isn't as frightening or risky as some would have you believe.

But it's a journey and **LET THE JOURNEY BEGIN.**

CHAPTER ONE

THE PERSONALITY OF AN ENTREPRENEUR

Every year, hundreds of thousands of people start their businesses. But while most succeed (yes, that's the truth!), many do fail. Why? One of the common causes of startup failure is **LACK OF PREPARATION.** Opportunity comes in many guises. It might be when potential customers start calling you, or perhaps a business in your area is failing and you know you can make it work. Or maybe you feel as if you're underemployed (working below your potential salary or your skill level) or not putting your skills and talents to their best use. Perhaps there's a need for the product or service you want to provide. Or you've simply figured out a better or a new way to do something. You have to be prepared to take a plunge.

You'll need to prepare for the responsibilities that come with business ownership. When things go wrong, the buck stops with you. You won't have the luxury of going home at 5 o'clock while the boss stays all night to fix a chaotic situation. Someone whose only desire is to get rich quick probably won't last long owning his or her own business.

Through surveys and research, it is known that successful entrepreneurs share some common personality traits, the most important of which is confidence. They possess confidence not only in themselves but also in their ability to sell their ideas, set up a business and trust their intuition along the way. Small business is fiercely competitive, and it's the business owners with confidence who survive.

Think you may have what it takes to be an entrepreneur? Here are five other personality traits entrepreneurs must have:

Passion. This is the most significant characteristic that every entrepreneur has, and for obvious reasons. They are successful because they love what they do. These entrepreneurs put all the extra efforts and hours they have into the business to make it successful and flourish. It is a pleasure for them to see the results of their labor, which goes well beyond the money received. People like this are always researching and reading things to find strategies in how they can make their business better.

As Steve Jobs once said, according to the Smithsonian Institution, "I'm convinced that about half of what separates the successful entrepreneurs from the non-successful ones is pure perseverance."

Motivation. Entrepreneurs have excellent communication skills for selling the products to their customers and motivating the employees. Yes, most entrepreneurs who have the power to motivate their employees can see their business grow within no time. These entrepreneurs are also great at instructing others to be successful and highlighting the advantages of any situation. They know how to communicate they dream and inspire others to join them on their journey to achieving it.

Determination. They are never greatly impacted by the defeats of an encounter. For them, failure is like an opening for a success story, and hence, they try again and again just till they get the success they are expecting. Moreover, these entrepreneurs are not wired to believe that some things are not possible and cannot be done.

Creativity. One of the main aspects of creativity is the ability to find a relationship between two unrelated situations or events. Entrepreneurs usually come up with solutions to these problems that are a combination of other things. These people normally re-purpose the items for marketing them to new industries.

Open-Minded. Entrepreneurs understand that each situation and event is a business opportunity. There are new ideas that continually come out regarding new potential businesses, people skills, efficiency, and workflows. These people can see all that is around them and direct the focus towards their objectives and goals.

Disciplined. Entrepreneurs always focus their energy on making the business work, and for eliminating the distractions or obstacles to their goals. Their overarching strategies help them to reach the goals they have while they outline the plan to achieve the outcome. Moreover, entrepreneurs become successful and become disciplined in taking new steps every day towards the accomplishment of their goals.

ASSESS YOUR STRENGTHS AND WEAKNESSES

One person rarely possesses all the qualities needed to be successful in business. Everyone has strong suits and weak points. What's important is to understand your strengths and weaknesses. To do this, you need to evaluate the major achievements in your personal and professional life and the skills you used to accomplish them.

The following steps can help:

Create a personal resume. Compose a resume that lists your professional and personal experiences as well as your expertise. For each job, describe the duties you were responsible for and the degree of your success. Include professional skills, educational background, hobbies and accomplishments that required expertise or special knowledge. When completed, this resume will give you a better idea of the kind of business that best suits your interests and experience.

Analyze your attributes. Are you friendly and self-motivated? Are you a hard worker? Are you well-organized? Evaluating your attributes reveals your likes and dislikes as well as strengths and weaknesses. If you don't feel comfortable around other people, then a business that requires a lot of customer interaction might not be right for you. Or you may want to hire a "people person" to handle customer service, while you concentrate on the tasks you do best.

Analyze your professional attributes. Small-business owners wear many different hats, but that doesn't mean you have to be a jack-of-all-trades. Just be aware of the areas where you're competent and the areas where you need help, such as sales, marketing, advertising and administration. Next to each function, record your competency level—excellent, good, fair or poor.

DEFINE YOUR GOALS

In addition to evaluating your strengths and weaknesses, it's important to define your business goals. For some people, the goal is the freedom to do what they want when they want, without anyone telling them otherwise. For others, the goal is financial security.

Setting goals is an integral part of choosing the business that's right for you. After all, if your business doesn't meet your personal goals, you probably won't be happy waking up each morning and trying to make the business a success. Sooner or later, you'll stop putting forth the effort needed to make the concept work. When setting goals, aim for the following qualities:

Specificity. You have a better chance of achieving a goal if it is specific. "Raising capital" isn't a specific goal; "raising $10,000 by July 1" is.

Optimism. Be positive when you set your goals. "Being able to pay the bills" isn't exactly an inspirational goal. "Achieving financial security" phrases your goal in a more positive manner, thus firing up your energy to attain it.

Realism. If you set a goal to earn $100,000 a month when you've never earned that much in a year, that goal is unrealistic. Begin with small steps, such as increasing your monthly income by 1 dollar or 10 dollars. Once your first goal is met, you can reach for larger ones

Short and long term. Short-term goals are attainable in a period of weeks to a year. Long-term goals can be for five, ten or even twenty years; they should be substantially greater than short-term goals but should still be realistic.

There are several factors to consider when setting goals:

Income. Many entrepreneurs go into business to achieve financial security. Consider how much money you want to make during your first year of operation and each year thereafter, up to five years.

Lifestyle. This includes areas such as travel, hours of work, investment of personal assets and geographic location. Are you willing to travel extensively or to move? How many hours are you willing to work? Which assets are you willing to risk?

Type of work. When setting goals for the type of work, you need to determine whether you like working outdoors, in an office, with computers, on the phone, with lots of people, with children and so on.

Ego gratification. Face it: Many people go into business to satisfy their egos. Owning a business can be very ego-gratifying, especially if you're in a business that's considered glamorous or exciting. You need to decide how important ego gratification is to you and what business best fills that need.

The most important rule of self-evaluation and goal-setting is honesty. Going into business with your eyes wide open about your strengths and weaknesses, your likes and dislikes and your ultimate goals let you confront the decisions you'll face with greater confidence and a greater chance of success.

Setting goals not only gives you an ongoing road map for success, but it shows you the best alternatives should you need or desire for a change along the way. You should review your goals regularly. Many do this daily as it helps them assess their progress and gives them the ability to make faster and more informed decisions. Take a few minutes to answer the following questions needed to reassess your goals. You'll find this very helpful in setting and resetting your goals.

The most important reason for being in business for myself is:

What I like best about being in business for myself is:

Within five years, I would like my business to be:

When I look back over the past five years of my career, I feel:

My financial condition as of today is:

I feel, the next thing I must do about my business is:

The most important part of my business is (or will be):

The area of my business I excel in is:

CHAPTER TWO

GETTING AN IDEA FOR YOUR BUSINESS

M any people believe starting a business is a mysterious process. They know they want to start a business, but they don't know the first steps to take. People always wonder if this is a good time to start their business idea. The fact is, there's never a bad time to launch a business.

Everyone has his or her roadblock, something that prevents them from taking the crucial first step. Most people are afraid to start; they may fear the unknown or failure, or even success. Others find starting something overwhelming in the mistaken belief they have to start from scratch. They think they have to come up with something that no one has ever done before a new invention, a unique service. In other words, they think they have to reinvent the wheel.

It's not the business you're in, but the way you do business, that makes the difference. Every business has a formula for making money. You need the determination to figure out the formula for your particular business. -- Greg Brophy.

Unless you are a tech guru, reinventing might be a waste of time. Most people starting a business may not be coming up with something so unique that no one has ever heard of but instead answering the questions: "How can I improve on this?" or "Can I do this better or different from the other guy doing it over there?" Or simply, "Is there market share not being served that makes room for another business in this category?"

START THE IDEA PROCESS

How do you start the idea process? First, take out a sheet of paper and across the top write "Things About Me." List five to seven personal things you like to do or that you're indeed good at, (We'll get to your work life in a minute).

Your list might include: "I'm good with people, I love kids, I love to read, I love computers, I love numbers, I'm good at coming up with marketing concepts, and I'm a problem solver."

Just write down whatever comes to your mind; it doesn't need to make sense. Once you have your list, number the items down one side of the paper.

On the other side of the paper, list things that you don't think you're good at or you don't like to do. Maybe you're good at marketing concepts, but you don't like to meet people, you're not that fond of kids, you don't like to do public speaking or you don't want to travel. Don't overthink it; just write down your thoughts. When completed, ask yourself: "If there were three to five products or services that would make my personal life better, what would they be?" This is your personal life as a man, woman, father, husband, mother, wife, parent, grandparent, whatever your situation may be. Determine what products or services would make your life easier or happier, make you more productive or efficient, or simply give you more time.

Next, ask yourself the same question about your business life. Examine what you like and dislike about your work life as well as what traits people like and dislike about you. Finally, ask yourself why you're seeking to start a business in the first place. Then, when you're done, look for a pattern to emerge (i.e., whether there's a need for a business doing one of the things you like or are good at).

Don't overlook publications in your search for business ideas. Books, newspapers and magazines all contain a wealth of ideas. Your reading list should include business, lifestyle, and niche publications like pets or antique tractors. Read your local newspaper, as well as major newspapers from the large trend-setting cities like Birmingham, London and San Francisco, many of which you can read online for free.

It is important to know that before you start a business, you have to examine the potential, that your product or service has, and whether the opportunity exists to make a good deal of money.

It may be a "hit and run" product, where you're going to get in, make a lot of money, and then get out. That's not necessarily a bad thing; fads have made some entrepreneurs incredibly wealthy. But remember, once you're in the fad business, it's hard to know when it's time to get out. And if you guess wrong or try to make a classic out of a fad, you're going to lose all the money you have earned.

You can glimpse new possibilities by ridding yourself of blocking assumptions. If we assume soap always comes in blocks, we will never be able to imagine it in liquid form. If we confine our thinking about crisps to potatoes, we will never imagine the possibility of parsnip and beetroot crisps. Likewise, when we think 'lock', we may automatically imagine 'key'. Locks may have keys but we have invented many different kinds of 'key', such as electronic cards. Many cities have broken the blocking assumption that big events such as football matches take place inside a stadium by opening up free space and exploiting the possibilities of wide-screen television.

Here are some start-up stories

Reed Hastings was inspired after he got a whopping $40 late charge, instead of getting mad, he got inspired. Hastings wondered "How come movie rentals don't work like a health club, where, whether you use it a lot or a little, you get charged the same?" From this thought, Netflix.com, an online DVD rental service, was born. From its start in 1999, Netflix has grown into a big business with revenues topping $1.3 billion. Getting an idea can be as simple as keeping your eyes peeled for the latest hot businesses; they crop up all the time.

The John Ferolito and Don Vultaggio way. Back in the 70s, a couple of Brooklyn friends started a beer distributor out of the back of an old VW bus. Two decades later, after seeing how well Snapple was doing they decided to try their hand at soft drinks and launched Arizona Green Tea. Today, Arizona teas are #1 in America and distributed worldwide. The friends still own the company.

The Joe Coulombe way. After operating a small chain of convenience stores in southern California, Joe Coulombe had an idea: that upwardly mobile college grads might want something better than 7-11. So he opened a tropical-themed market in Pasadena, stocked it with good wine and booze, hired good people, and paid them well. He added more locations near universities, then healthy foods, and that's how Trader Joe's got started.

You can take any idea and customize it to soothe the present time and your community. Add your creativity to any concept. Customizing a concept isn't a choice; it's a necessity if you want your business to be successful. You can't just take an idea, plop it down and say "OK, this is it." Outside of a McDonald's, Subway or other major franchise concepts, there are very few businesses that work with a one-size-fits-all approach.

One of the best ways to determine whether your idea will succeed in your community is to talk to people you know. If it's a business idea, talk to co-workers and colleagues. Run personal ideas by your family or neighbors. Don't be afraid of people stealing your idea. It's just not likely. Just discuss the general concept; you don't need to spill all the details.

CHAPTER THREE

DETERMINE THE RIGHT BUSINESS

Hopefully, by now, the process of determining what business is right for you has at least been somewhat demystified. Understand that business startup isn't rocket science. No, it isn't easy to begin a business, but it's not as complicated or as scary as many people think, either.

It's a step by step, common-sense procedure. So take it a step at a time.

First step: Figure out what you want to do. Once you have the idea, talk to people to find out what they think. Ask *"Would you buy and/or use this, and how much would you pay?"*

Understand that many people around you won't encourage you (some will even discourage you) to pursue your entrepreneurial journey. Some will tell you they have your best interests at heart; they just want you to see the reality of the situation. Some will envy your courage; others will resent you for having the guts to do something. You can't allow these naysayers to dissuade you, to stop your journey before it even begins.

Once you get an idea for a business, what's the most important trait you need as an entrepreneur? *Perseverance*. When you set out to launch your business, you'll be told "no" more times than you've ever been told before. You can't take it personally; you've got to get beyond the "no" and move on to the next person because eventually, you're going to get to a "yes."

One of the most common warnings you'll hear is about the risk. Everyone will tell you it's risky to start your own business. Sure, starting a business is risky, but what in life isn't? Plus, there's a difference between foolish risks and calculated ones. If you carefully consider what you're doing, get help when you need it, and never stop asking questions, you can mitigate your risk.

Determining what you want to do is only the first step. You've still got a lot of homework to do, a lot of research in front of you. Buying this book is a smart first step. Most important: Do something.

Don't sit back year after year and say "This is the year I'm going to start my business." Make this the year you do it!

DETERMINE THE APPROPRIATE TIME

As with any business, your plan of attack should start with a thorough assessment of your idea's market potential. Often, this step alone will be enough to tell you whether you should start **part-time or full time.** You can't become so caught up in your love for what you're doing that you overlook the business realities. If you find there is a huge unmet need for your product or service, no major competition and a ready supply of eager customers, then, by all means, go ahead and start full time. If, on the other hand, you find that the market won't support a full-time business, but might someday with proper marketing and business development, then it is probably best to start part-time at first.

Starting part-time offers several advantages. It reduces your risk because you can rely on income and benefits from your full-time job. Starting part-time also allows your business to grow gradually. Perhaps the biggest problem for part-time entrepreneurs is the risk of burnout. Holding down a full-time job while running a part-time business leaves you with little, if any, leisure time; as a result, your personal and family life may suffer. That's not to say a part-time business can't work. It can if you have excellent time management skills, strong self-discipline, and support from family and friends. Also crucial is your commitment: "Don't think that, since you already have a job, you don't have to work hard at your business. You must have a plan of attack."

FACTORS TO CONSIDER WHEN STARTING A BUSINESS

Family Affairs. The emotional and psychological side of starting a business is less cut and dried than financial and market aspects, but it's just as important in your decision to start part-time or full time. Begin by discussing the situation with your spouse, significant other or family members. Do they support your decision to start a business? Do they understand the sacrifices both full-time and part-time businesses will require from you, from them and the whole family? Make sure your loved ones feel free to bring any objections or worries out in the open. The time to do this is now not three months after you have committed to your business and it is too late to back out.

Then, work together to come up with practical solutions to the problems you foresee (could your spouse take over some of the household chores you currently handle, for example). Lay some ground rules for the part-time business, for instance, no work on Sunday afternoons, or no discussing business at the dinner table.

To make your part-time business success and keep your family happy, time management is key. Balance the hours you have available. Get up early, and don't spend valuable time on frivolous phone calls and other time-wasters.

Getting Personal. Besides, the effect business ownership will have on your family, equally important to consider is the toll it might take on you. If the idea of taking the full-time business plunge and giving up your comfy salary and cushy benefits keeps you awake at night biting your nails, then perhaps a part-time business is best. On the other hand, if you need to work long hours at your current full-time job, you commute 60 miles round-trip and you have 2-year-old triplets, piling a part-time business on top of all those commitments could be the straw that breaks the camel's back.

Of course, a full-time business does require long, long hours, but a part-time business combined with a full-time job can be even more stressful. If this is the route you're considering, carefully assess the effects on your life. You'll be using evenings, weekends and lunch hours and, most likely, your holidays, sick days and vacation time to take care of business. You may probably have to give up leisure activities such as going to the movies, watching TV, reading or going to the gym. How will you feel the next time you drag yourself home, exhausted after a late night at the office, then have to sit right down and spend four hours working on a project that a client needs the next morning? This is the kind of commitment you will need to make if you expect your part-time business to succeed. Carefully consider whether you have the mental and physical stamina to give your best effort to both your job and your business.

Financial Plan. One major factor in the decision to start part-time or full time is your financial situation. Before launching a full-time business, most experts recommend putting aside enough to live on for at least six months to a year. (That amount may vary; completing your business plan will show you in detail how long you can expect to wait before your business begins earning a profit.)

Basic factors you should consider includes the amount of your existing savings, whether you have assets that could be sold for cash, whether friends or family members might offer you financing or loans, and whether your spouse or other family members' salaries could be enough to support your family while you launch a business full time.

If, like many people, you lack the financial resources to start full time, beginning part-time is often a good alternative. However, even if you do start part-time, you'll want to keep some figures in mind. Specifically, how do you know when your business is making enough money that you can say goodbye to your day job?

A good rule of thumb is to wait until your part-time business is bringing in income equivalent to at least 30 per cent of your current salary from your full-time job. Another good idea is to start putting more money aside while you still have your day job. That way, when you take the full-time plunge, you'll have a financial cushion to supplement the income from your business

Market aspects. Investigate factors such as the competition in your industry, the economy in your area, the demographic breakdown of your client base, and the availability of potential customers. If you are thinking of opening an upscale beauty salon, for example, evaluate the number of similar shops in operation, as well as the number of affluent women in the area and the fees they are willing to pay. Once you have determined there is a need for your business, outline your goals and strategies in a comprehensive business plan.

You should always conduct extensive research, make market projections for your business, and set goals for yourself based on these findings. It gives you a tremendous view of the long-range possibilities and keeps the business on the right track. Don't neglect writing a business plan even if you're starting part-time: A well-written business plan will help you take your business full time later on.

Doing your market research and business plan will give you a more realistic idea of whether your business can work part-time. If you've got your heart set on a business that traditionally requires a full-time commitment, think creatively: There may be ways to make it work on a part-time basis.

Finally, whether to start part-time or full time is a decision only you can make. Whichever route you take, the secret to success is an honest assessment of your resources, your commitment level and the support systems you have in place. With the above factors firmly in mind, you will be able to make the right choice. Decide to start a business later.

SECTION TWO
THE PLANNING STAGE

You've come up with a great idea for a business but you're not ready to kick it off. Before you go any further, the next step is figuring out who your market is, creating good niche and writing a mission statement for your business.

CHAPTER FOUR

DEFINE YOUR MARKET

There are two basic markets you can sell to; consumer and business. These divisions are fairly obvious. For example, if you are selling women's clothing from a retail store, your target market is consumers; if you are selling office supplies, your target market is businesses (this is referred to as "B2B" sales). In some cases for example, if you run a printing business you may be marketing to both businesses and individual consumers.

No business, particularly a small one can be all things to all people. The more narrowly you can define your target market, the better. This process is known as creating a niche and is key to success for even the big companies. Walmart and Tiffany are both retailers, but they have very different niches: Walmart caters to bargain-minded shoppers, while Tiffany appeals to upscale jewelry consumers.

Good niches do not just fall into your lap; they must be very carefully crafted.

Rather than creating a niche, many entrepreneurs make the mistake of falling into the "all over the map" trap, claiming they can do many things and be good at all of them. These people quickly learn a tough lesson, *Falkenstein warns: "Smaller is bigger in business, and smaller is not all over the map; it's highly focused."*

CRAFTING A GOOD NICHE

Creating a good niche involves following a seven-step process:

Make a wish list. With whom do you want to do business? Be as specific as you can: Identify the geographic range and the types of businesses or customers you want your business to target. If you don't know whom you want to do business with, you can't make contact. You must recognize that you can't do business with everybody. Otherwise, you risk exhausting yourself and confusing your customers. These days, the trend is toward smaller niches. For example, targeting teenagers isn't specific enough; targeting male, African American teenagers with family incomes of 75,000 and up is. Aiming at companies that sell software is too broad; aiming at New York-based companies that provide internet software sales and training and have sales of $15 million or more is a better goal.

Focus. Clarify what you want to sell, remembering: a) you can't be all things to all people and b) "smaller is bigger." Your niche is not the same as the field in which you work. For example, a retail clothing business is not a niche but a field. A more specific niche may be "maternity clothes for executive women."

To begin this focusing process, these techniques will help you:

Make a list of things you do best and the skills implicit in each of them.

List your achievements.

Identify the most important lessons you have learned in life.

Look for patterns that reveal your style or approach to resolving problems.

Your niche should arise naturally from your interests and experience. For example, if you spent ten years working in a consulting firm, but also spent ten years working for a small, family-owned business, you may decide to start a consulting business that specializes in small, family-owned companies.

Describe the customer's worldview. When you look at the world from your prospective customers' perspective, you can identify their needs or wants. The best way to do this is to talk to prospective customers and identify their main concerns. We will discuss this later

Synthesize. At this stage, your niche should begin to take shape as your ideas and the client's needs and wants to coalesce to create something new. A good niche has five qualities:

It takes you where you want to go in other words, it conforms to your long-term vision.

Somebody else wants it namely, customers.

It's carefully planned.

It's one-of-a-kind, the "only game in town."

It evolves, allowing you to develop different profit centers and still retain the core business, thus ensuring long-term success.

27

Evaluate. Now it's time to evaluate your proposed product or service against the five criteria in the synthesize stage. Perhaps you'll find that the niche you had in mind requires more business travel than you're ready for. That means it doesn't fulfill one of the above criteria—it won't take you where you want to go. So scrap it, and move on to the next idea.

Test. Once you have a match between niche and product, test-market it. "Allow people to buy your product or service not just theoretically but putting it out there," This can be done by offering samples, such as a free mini-seminar or a sample copy of your newsletter. The test shouldn't cost you a lot of money: "If you spend huge amounts of money on the initial market test, you are probably doing it wrong," she says.

Go for it! It's time to implement your idea. For many entrepreneurs, this is the most difficult stage. But fear not: If you did your homework, entering the market will be a calculated risk, not just a gamble.

Re-niching. Once your niche is established and well-received by your market, you may be tempted to rest on your laurels. That's not a good idea. You must keep growing by re-niching. This doesn't mean changing your focus, but rather further adapting it to the environment around you." Ask yourself the following questions when you think you have found your niche and ask them again every six months or so to make sure your niche is still on target:

Who are your target clients?

Who aren't your target clients?

Do you refuse certain kinds of business if it falls outside your niche?

What do clients think you stand for?

Is your niche in a constant state of evolution?

Does your niche offer what prospective customers want?

Do you have a plan and delivery system that effectively conveys the need for your niche to the right market?

Can you confidently predict the life cycle of your niche?

How can your niche be expanded into a variety of products or services that act as profit centers?

Do you have a sense of passion and focused energy with respect to your niche?

Does your niche feel comfortable and natural?

How will pursuing your niche contribute to achieving the goals you have set for your business?

Creating a niche is the difference between being in business and not being in business. It's the difference between surviving and thriving, between just liking what you do and the joy of success."

CHAPTER FIVE

CREATE A MISSION STATEMENT

A key tool that can be as important as your business plan is the mission statement, it captures, in a few succinct sentences, the essence of your business's goals and the philosophies underlying them. Equally important, the mission statement signals what your business is all about to your customers, employees, suppliers and the community.

The mission statement reflects every facet of your business: the range and nature of the products you offer, pricing, quality, service, marketplace position, growth potential, use of technology, and your relationships with your customers, employees, suppliers, competitors and the community.

Consider the statement one entrepreneur developed for her consulting business: "ABC Enterprises is a company devoted to developing human potential. Our mission is to help people create innovative solutions and make informed choices to improve their lives. We motivate and encourage others to achieve personal and professional fulfillment. Our motto is: Together, we believe that the best in each of us enriches all of us."

Answering the following ten questions will help you to create a verbal picture of your business's mission:

1. **Why are you in business?** What do you want for yourself, your family and your customers? Think about the spark that ignited your decision to start a business. What will keep it burning?

2. **Who are your customers?** What can you do for them that will enrich their lives and contribute to their success now and in the future?

3. **What image of your business do you want to convey?** Customers, suppliers, employees and the public will all have perceptions of your company. How will you create the desired picture?

29

4. **What is the nature of your products and services?** What factors determine pricing and quality? Consider how these relate to the reasons for your business's existence. How will all this change over time?

5. **What level of service do you provide?** Most companies believe they offer "the best service available," but do your customers agree? Don't be vague; define what makes your service so extraordinary.

6. **What roles do you and your employees play?** Wise captains develop a leadership style that organizes, challenges and recognizes employees.

7. **What kind of relationships will you maintain with suppliers?** Every business is in partnership with its suppliers. When you succeed, so do they.

8. **How do you differ from your competitors?** Many entrepreneurs forget they are pursuing the same dollars as their competitors. What do you do better, cheaper or faster than competitors? How can you use competitors' weaknesses to your advantage?

9. **How will you use technology, capital, processes, products and services to reach your goals?** A description of your strategy will keep your energies focused on your goals.

10. **What underlying philosophies or values guided your responses to the previous questions?** Some businesses choose to list these separately. Writing them down clarifies the "why" behind your mission.

Tips to make your mission statement the best it can be:

Involve those connected to your business. Even if you are a sole proprietor, it helps to get at least one other person's ideas for your mission statement. Other people can help you see strengths, weaknesses and voids you might miss. If you have no partners or investors to include, consider knowledgeable family members and close friends, employees or accountants. Be sure, however, to pick only positive, supportive people who truly want you to succeed.

Set aside several hours, a full day, if possible to work on your statement. Mission statements are short typically more than one sentence but rarely exceeding a page. Still, writing one is not a short process. It takes time to come up with language that simultaneously describes an organization's heart and soul and serves as an inspirational beacon to everyone involved in the business. Large corporations often spend an entire weekend crafting a statement.

Plan a date. Set aside time to meet with the people who'll be helping you. Write a list of topics to discuss or think about. Find a quiet, comfortable place away from phones and interruptions.

Be prepared. If you have several people involved, be equipped with refreshments, extra lists of topics, paper and pencils. Because not everyone understands what a mission statement is about, explain its meaning and purpose before you begin.

Brainstorm. Consider every idea, no matter how silly it sounds. Stimulate ideas by looking at sample mission statements and thinking about or discussing the 10 questions stated on the previous page. If you're working with a group, use a flip chart to record responses so everyone can see them. Once you've finished brainstorming, ask everyone to write individual mission statements for your business. Read the statements, select the best bits and pieces, and fit them together.

Use radiant words. Once you have the basic idea in writing, polish the language of your mission statement. The statement should create dynamic, visual images and inspire action. Use offbeat, colorful verbs and adjectives to spice up your statement. Don't hesitate to drop in words like "kaleidoscope," "sizzle," "cheer," "outrageous" and "marvel" to add zest. If you want customers to "boast" about your goods and services, then say so along with the reasons why. Some businesses include a glossary that defines the terms used in the statement.

Once your mission statement is complete, start spreading the word! You need to convey your mission statement to others inside and outside the business to tell everyone you know where you are going and why. Post it in your office where you, your employees and visitors can see it every day. Print it on the company materials, such as your brochures and your business plan or even on the back of your business cards.

When you're launching a new business, you can't afford to lose sight of your objectives. By always keeping your mission statement in front of you, you'll keep your goals in mind and ensure smooth sailing.

CHAPTER SIX

CONDUCTING MARKET RESEARCH

Wait! Before you shift into high gear, you must determine whether there really is a market for your product or service. Not only that, but you also need to ascertain what if any fine-tuning is needed. Quite simply, you must conduct market research.

Many business owners neglect this crucial step in product development for the sole reason that they don't want to hear any negative feedback. They are convinced their product or service is perfect just the way it is, and they don't want to risk tampering with it. As an entrepreneur, you must be able to decipher when constructive criticism and negative feedback are given. Feedbacks allows you to perform better and properly redefine your approach.

Other entrepreneurs bypass market research because they fear it will be too expensive. With all the other startup costs you're facing, it's not easy to justify spending money on research that will only prove what you knew all along: Your product is a winner. Regardless of the reason, failing to do market research can amount to a death sentence for your product.

Consider market research an investment in your future. If you make the necessary adjustments to your product or service now, you'll save money in the long run. Whether you hire a professional market research firm or take on the task yourself, your market research should clearly answer the following questions:

Who will buy my product or service?

Why will they buy it?

Where will they buy it, specialty shops, department stores, mail order?

What do I need to charge to make a healthy profit?

What products or services will mine be competing with?

Am I positioning my product or service correctly? (In other words, if there's a lot of competition, look for a specialized market niche.)

What government regulations will my product or service be subject to?

WHY MARKET RESEARCH...

Market research is a way of collecting information you can use to solve or avoid marketing problems. Good market research gives you the data you need to develop a marketing plan that works for you. It enables you to identify the specific segments within a market that you want to target and to create an identity for your product or service that separates it from your competitors.

Market research can also help you choose the best geographic location in which to launch your new business. Before you start your market research, it's a good idea to meet with a consultant, talk to a business or marketing professor at a local college or university, or contact your local SBA district office. These sources can offer guidance and help you with the first step in market research: deciding exactly what information you need to gather.

As a rule of thumb, market research should provide you with information about three critical areas: the industry, the consumer and the competition.

Industry information. In researching the industry, look for the latest trends. Compare the statistics and growth in the industry. What areas of the industry appear to be expanding, and what areas are declining? Is the industry catering to new types of customers? What technological developments are affecting the industry? How can you use them to your advantage? A thriving, stable industry is key; you don't want to start a new business in a field that is on the decline.

Consumer side. On the consumer side, your market research should begin with a market survey. A thorough market survey will help you make a reasonable sales forecast for your new business. To do a market survey, you first need to determine the market limits or physical boundaries of the area to which your business sells. Next, study the spending characteristics of the population within this location. Estimate the location's purchasing power, based on its per capita income, its median income level, the unemployment rate, population and other demographic factors. Determine the current sales volume in the area for the type of product or service you will sell. Finally, estimate how much of the total sales volume you can reasonably obtain. (This last step is extremely important. Opening your new business in a given community won't necessarily generate additional business volume; it may simply redistribute the business that's already there.)

Competition close-up. Based on a combination of industry research and consumer research, a clearer picture of your competition will emerge. Do not underestimate the number of competitors out there. Keep an eye out for potential future competitors as well as current ones.

Examine the number of competitors on a local and, if relevant, national scale. Study their strategies and operations. Your analysis should supply a clear picture of potential threats, opportunities, and the weaknesses and strengths of the competition facing your new business. When looking at the competition, try to see what trends have been established in the industry and whether there's an opportunity or advantage for your business. Use the library, the internet and other secondary research sources described later in this chapter to research competitors. Read as many articles as you can on the companies you will be competing with. If you are researching publicly owned companies, contact them and obtain copies of their annual reports. These often show not only how successful a company is, but also what products or services it plans to emphasize in the future.

One of the best websites for researching the competition is Hoover's Online (hoovers.com), which, for a fee, provides in-depth profiles of more than 43,000 companies. However, there is also free content available, plus you can try a free trial subscription. You can also gather information on competing businesses by visiting them in person. Take along a questionnaire

MARKET RESEARCH METHODS

In conducting your market research, you will gather two types of data: primary and secondary.

Primary research is information that comes directly from the source that is, potential customers. You can compile this information yourself or hire someone else to gather it for you via surveys, focus groups and other methods. *Secondary research* involves gathering statistics, reports, studies and other data from organizations such as government agencies, trade associations and your local chamber of commerce. The vast majority of research you can find will be secondary research. While large companies spend huge amounts of money on market research, the good news is that plenty of information is available for free to entrepreneurs on a tight budget. The best places to start? Your local library and the internet.

Your industry trade association can offer a wealth of information such as market statistics, lists of members, and books and reference materials. Talking to others in your association can be one of the most valuable ways of gaining informal data about a region or customer base.

Government agencies are an invaluable source of market research, most of it free. Almost every county government publishes population density and distribution figures in widely available census tracts. These publications will show you the number of people living in specific areas, such as precincts, water districts or even ten-block neighborhoods. Some counties publish reports on population trends that show the population ten years ago, five years ago and today. Watch out for a static, declining or small population; ideally, you want to locate where there is an expanding population that wants your products and services.

Local colleges and universities are valuable sources of information. Many college business departments have students who are eager to work in the "real world," gathering information and doing research at little or no cost. Finally, local business schools are a great source of experts. Many business professors do consult on the side, and some will even be happy to offer you marketing, sales, strategic planning or financial information for free. Call professors who specialize in these areas; if they can't help, they'll be able to put you in touch with someone who can.

Community Organizations; Your local chamber of commerce or business development agency can supply useful information. They are usually free of charge, including assistance with site selection, demographic reports, and directories of local businesses. They may also offer seminars on marketing and related topics that can help you do better research.

Financial and business services firm D&B offers a range of reference sources that can help startups. Some of the information they offer as part of their Sales & Marketing Solutions are directories for career opportunities, consultants, service companies and regional businesses. Visit their website at dnb.com for more information.

Going Online; These days, entrepreneurs can conduct much of their market research without ever leaving their computers, thanks to the universe of online services and information. Start with the major consumer online services, which offer access to business databases. You can find everything from headline and business news to industry trends and company-specific business information, such as a firm's address, telephone number, a field of business and the name of the CEO. This information is critical for identifying prospects, developing mailing lists and planning sales calls. ***Here are a few to get you started:***

KnowThis.com's (knowthis.com) marketing virtual library includes a tab on the site called "Weblinks" that contains links to a wide variety of market research web resources.

BizMiners.com (bizminers.com) lets you choose national market research reports for 16,000 industries in 300 U.S. markets, local research reports for 16,000 industries in 250 metro markets, or financial profiles for 10,000 U.S. industries. The reports are available online for a nominal cost.

MarketResearch.com (marketresearch.com) has more than 250,000 research reports from hundreds of sources consolidated into one accessible collection that's updated daily. No subscription fee is required, and you pay only for the parts of the report you need with its "Buy by the Section" feature. After paying the information is delivered online to your personal library on the site.

All the sources mentioned earlier (trade associations, government agencies) should also have websites you can visit to get information quickly. If you don't have time to investigate online services yourself, consider hiring an information broker to find the information you need. Information brokers gather information quickly. They can act as a small company's research arm, identifying the most accurate and cost-effective information sources.

Note "The time when you need to do something is when no one else is willing to do it when people are saying it can't be done." - Mary Frances Berry.

CHAPTER SEVEN

NAME YOUR BUSINESS

The right name can make your company the talk of the town; the wrong one can doom it to obscurity and failure. It is okay to put just as much effort into naming your business just as you did into coming up with your idea, writing your business plan and selecting a market and location. Ideally, your name should convey the expertise, value and uniqueness of the product or service you have developed. In reality, any name can be effective if it's backed by the appropriate marketing strategy.

I have learned that success is to be measured not so much by the position that one has reached in life as by the obstacles overcome while trying to succeed." - Booker Washington

If you can spare the money from your startup budget, professional help could be a solid investment. After all, the name you choose now will affect your marketing plans for the duration of your business. If you're like most business owners, though, the responsibility for thinking up a name will be all your own. The good news is by following the same basic steps professional namers use, you can come up with a meaningful moniker that works without breaking the bank.

COMMUNICATE WITH YOUR NAME

To be most effective, your company name should reinforce the key elements of your business. Your work in developing a niche and a mission statement will help you pinpoint the elements you want to emphasize in your name. Consider retail as an example. In retailing, the market is so segmented that a name must convey very quickly what the customer is going after. For example, if it's a warehouse store, it has to convey that impression. If it's an upscale store selling high-quality foods, it has to convey that impression. The name combined with the logo is very important in doing that. So the first and most important step in choosing a name is deciding what your business is.

One common naming error that can be fatal to a new business: choosing a name that's difficult to pronounce. If people don't know how to pronounce your business name, they will be hesitant to say it. That means they're less likely to tell friends about your company or to ask for your product by name.

Should your name be meaningful? Most experts say yes. The more your name communicates to consumers, the less effort you must exert to explain it. According to naming experts, name developers should give priority to real words or combinations of words over fabricated words. People prefer words they can relate to and understand. That's why professional namers universally condemn strings of numbers or initials as a bad choice.

Naming experts warns that business owners need to beware of names that are too narrowly defined.

Common pitfalls are geographic names or generic names. Take the name "San Pablo Disk Drives" as a hypothetical example. What if the company wants to expand beyond the city of San Pablo, California? What meaning will that name have for consumers in Chicago or Pittsburgh? And what if the company diversifies beyond disk drives into software or computer instruction manuals?

Before you start coming up with names for your new business, try to define the qualities that you want your business to be identified with. If you're starting a hearth-baked bread shop, you might want a name that conveys freshness, warmth and a homespun atmosphere. Immediately, you can see that names like "Kathy's Bread Shop" or "Arlington Breads" would communicate none of these qualities. But consider the name "Open Hearth Breads." The bread sounds homemade, hot and just out of the oven. Moreover, if you diversified your product line, you could alter the name to "Open Hearth Bakery." This change would enable you to hold on to your suggestive name without totally mystifying your established clientele.

THE DO'S AND DON'T

When choosing a business name, keep the following tips in mind:

Choose a name that appeals not only to you but also to the kind of customers you are trying to attract.

To get customers to respond to your business on an emotional level, choose a comforting or familiar name that conjures up pleasant memories.

Don't pick a name that is long or confusing.

Stay away from cute puns that only you understand.

Don't use the word "Inc." after your name unless your company is incorporated.

Don't use the word "Enterprises" after your name; this term is often used by amateurs.

BRAINSTORMING FOR NAMES

Begin brainstorming, looking in dictionaries, books and magazines to generate ideas. Get friends and relatives to help if you like; the more minds, the merrier. Think of as many workable names as you can during this creative phase. Professional naming firms start with a raw base of 800 to 1,000 names and work from there. You probably don't have time to think of that many, but try to come up with at least 10 names that you feel good about. By the time you examine them from all angles, you'll eliminate at least half.

Other considerations depend on more individual factors. For instance, if you're thinking about marketing your business globally or if you are located in a multilingual area, you should make sure that your new name has no negative connotations in other languages. On another note, if your primary means of advertising will be in the telephone directory, you might favor names that are closer to the beginning of the alphabet. Finally, make sure that your name is in no way embarrassing. Put on the mind of a child and tinker with the letters a little. If none of your doodlings makes you snicker, it's probably OK.

A naming firm Interbrand advises name seekers to take a close look at their competition: The major function of a name is to distinguish your business from others. You have to weigh who's out there already, what type of branding approaches they have taken, and how you can use a name to separate yourself.

Testing, Testing

After you've narrowed the field to, say, four or five names that are memorable, expressive and can be read by the average grade-schooler, you are ready to do a trademark search. Must every name be trademarked? No. Many small businesses don't register their business names. As long as your state government gives you the go-ahead, you may operate under an unregistered business name for as long as you like assuming, of course, that you aren't infringing on anyone else's trade name.

But what if you are? Imagine either of these two scenarios: You are a brand-new manufacturing business just about to ship your first orders. An obscure little company in Ogunquit, Maine, considers the name of your business an infringement on their trademark and engages you in a legal battle that bankrupts your company. Or envision your business in five years. It's a thriving, growing concern, and you are contemplating expansion. But just as you are about to launch your franchise program, you learn that a small competitor in Modesto, California, has the same name, rendering your name unusable.

To illustrate the risk you run of treading on an existing trademark with your new name, consider this: When NameLab took on the task of renaming a chain of auto parts stores, they uncovered 87,000 names already in existence for stores of this kind. That's why even the smallest businesses should at least consider having their business names screened. You never know where your corner store is going to lead. If running a corner store is all a person is going to do, then there's no need to do a trademark search. But that local business may become a big business someday if that person has any ambition.

FINAL STEP

If you're lucky, you'll end up with three to five names that pass all your tests. How do you make your final decision? Recall all your initial criteria. Which name best fits your objectives? Which name most accurately describes the company you have in mind? Which name do you like the best? Every company arrives at a final decision in its way. Some entrepreneurs go with their gut or use personal reasons for choosing one name over another. Others are more scientific. Some companies do consumer research or testing with focus groups to see how the names are perceived. Others might decide that their name is going to be most important seen on the back of a truck, so they have a graphic designer turn the various names into logos to see which works best as a design element. Use any or all of these criteria. You can do it informally: Ask other people's opinions. Doodle an idea of what each name will look like on a sign or business stationery. Read each name aloud, paying attention to the way it sounds if you foresee radio advertising or telemarketing in your future.

CHAPTER EIGHT

THE 13 MAIN REASONS WHY NEW BUSINESSES FAIL

E ntrepreneurship statistics often vary. Some estimates claim that up to 95% of new businesses fail within five years. Others say the number is around 65%. Either way, these are staggering figures when one takes into account that most new businesses fail for more or less the same reasons. Most of these reasons are presented below ranked in the order of the threat they pose. Note, however, that those placed at the end of the list are not the least dangerous. It, therefore, makes sense to do as much as possible to avoid all of them.

INADEQUATE PLANNING
As simple as it sounds, lack of forethought and planning is the main culprit behind virtually every business failure. Thankfully, 75% of most business ideas fail on paper (i.e.: the planning stage), which is exactly where a business idea should fail. The only other option is to collapse on the street, perhaps under a pile of debt. Inadequate planning includes (but is not limited to), not fully understanding a product or service before selling it, not conducting detailed market or labor research, not compiling a realistic customer profile, not researching the competition, not selecting a proper business model, not determining all costs beforehand, or, in general, not doing enough preliminary work to determine if all the numbers add up. In short, running a business without a well-researched plan is like hacking through a jungle with a map. Put it this way, if you don't have the time or inclination to plan, write down, investigate, and analyze what it is you want to do in regards to starting a business, then you probably don't have what it takes to succeed in that business.

UNDERESTIMATING THE COMMITMENT IT TAKES TO SUCCEED
In a world where almost everything is wanted on a silver platter the moment, it's demanded, it's easy to forget that quality and strength take time to acquire.

For example, it can take up to six months or longer to put together a business plan and as much as five to seven years (or longer) to establish a solid customer base.

I'll use the story of the photocopier to illustrate this point.

The idea of photocopying text instead of making copies by hand was the brainchild of Chester Carlson, a visionary who developed his first successful machine-made 'dry writing' image in 1939. Over the years Carlson offered his idea to over 20 companies including GE, IBM, and Kodak, yet each turned the invention down by explaining that photocopiers weren't needed because carbon paper was good enough. Much to his credit, Carlson persisted eventually winning over the president of a small photographic paper company (Joe Wilson) who agreed to fund the development of what he saw as a promising new idea. Through thick and thin Mr Wilson kept his word, faithfully supporting Carlson even when he could not afford to do so. At one point, during the winter of 1959-1960, a team of engineers worked 24 hours a day, seven days a week to meet a deadline. With Wilson and Carlson unable to pay the heating bills, the men huddled around the prototype as they worked, wearing coats and boots (and with a blanket draped over themselves and the machine) to keep warm. The result was the launch of Xerox, a company that reached $1-billion in sales faster than any other business in history up to then. It took over 20 years and brought several people to the brink of financial ruin, but persistence, dedication and a good idea paid off.

CASH FLOW PROBLEMS

If passion, commitment, and planning are more important than money then why do cash flow problems appear at the top of a 'reasons why business fail' list? Think of it this way: money isn't needed to conceive a baby, but once a baby is born it needs to be fed and the bigger a baby gets the more food it needs. This is the same for a business. Too many entrepreneurs confuse the word cash with the word profit, thinking that they're the same. 'Profit' is a word for accountants. 'Cash' is what a business feeds on to survive. Employees, banks, and many suppliers must be paid in cash, not profit percentages. Any business can declare bankruptcy if finances are not properly managed.

Suggestions for improving cash flow include:

Don't go on a spending spree during the first year or two of operations. No matter how successful your business appears, or how enthusiastic you are to make improvements, the first year of operations is not the best time to spend money. It's time for collecting money. Avoid the temptation to celebrate or spend a lot of money during the first year or two of operations.

Before accepting credit from anyone, ask for and check credit references. Some banks will do this for you. Credit-checking services are available in most countries so take advantage of them!

Bill promptly. When possible, always ask for cash upfront when selling a product or service. Otherwise, set up a regular billing system, clearly state your terms, or negotiate with customers for payment in advance.

Create an incentive for receiving prompt payments. Offering customers a discount of 1% or 2% if they pay within ten days often provides a big incentive for them to do so.

Reduce inventory. Determine how much inventory your business needs and cut back on stock.

Consolidate your loans. If you've borrowed money from several different sources, consider taking out one big loan that covers them all. This may involve stretching out your payments for another year or two (thereby costing more in the long run), but if you need to lower your monthly expenditures it may be a good option.

Learn to barter. Sometimes products or services can be exchanged without money changing hands. For example, many years ago, a gym owner was convinced to expand his hours of operation by bringing in students that needed to do internships. Local university rules forbid the paying of interns so any company that 'hired' one received free labor in return for providing the student with some work experience.

POOR MANAGEMENT

Entrepreneurship is the death of management. Paradoxically, it's also been said that management is the death of entrepreneurship. What these comments refer to is the belief that after setting up business too many entrepreneurs stiffen into rigid managers that are guided by routines; a problem that probably arises because most people don't know what good management is about. In short, management is not about being a boss. Good management is about serving others: providing for others, motivating people, getting work done through others, and streamlining a business toward making a sale and that's just the beginning. Indeed, some practitioners believe that managers in denial of what's going on in their business are the real number one reason why most businesses fail.

Additional managerial problems include an inability to delegate, inflexibility, micro-managing the work of others, or abdicating important work responsibilities. Fortunately, it doesn't take a genius to be a good manager.

For the most part, competent management involves being curious and open-minded, having a good attitude, adopting adequate organization skills, offering quality training to employees, listening to others, being flexible to new ideas (i.e.: remaining entrepreneurial), harboring a hatred of the status quo, and instilling a business with a can-do attitude that may involve breaking the rules (but not the law).

43

NOT UNDERSTANDING THE IMPORTANCE OF CUSTOMERS

Setting up a new business involves so much work that it's easy to forget about paying customers. Interior design, bookkeeping, product displays and other non-revenue producing activities although important - should not be the priority of a business. Successful business operations are reliant upon receiving money from satisfied customers regularly. Your customers are an important part of your business.

STAFFING PROBLEMS

No matter what the business, finding honest workers who share the owner's passion and commitment can be an arduous and time-consuming process. As an entrepreneur, you may not be able to pay your employees more than your competitors, but you can certainly give them more. Employees should be trained properly and be made to feel useful because people work harder and show more commitment when they feel that they belong to an organization and are being listened to. In any business, employees come and go for any number of reasons, but it only makes sense to try and keep the good ones for as long as possible; high employee turnover is expensive, time-consuming, and draining.

INFLEXIBILITY

Small businesses should not act like rigid, inflexible corporations. From the business plan to the marketing campaign to the importance of finalizing a sale, if something isn't right it should be changed quickly. Change can happen in one of two ways: it can either be done by you or it can be used to run over you. Examples of inflexibility in business include not deferring to customer demands, feeling invincible against competitors, and refusing to acknowledge changes in technology, markets, or work practices.

POOR MARKETING AND/OR AN INABILITY TO SELL

Contrary to popular belief, if you build a better mousetrap the world will not beat a path to your door. Equally as true is that good products and services do not sell themselves. Simply put, the success of every enterprise hinges on its ability to sell and an ability to sell begins by understanding the basics of marketing, promotion, and human psychology. Additional problems associated with poor marketing and selling include relying too much on one particular customer, not focusing on a particular market segment, not undergoing sales training, and ignoring the competition (every business is always competing against something even if it's just a customer's time).

To remain solvent, a business must be able to successfully; announce to potential customers what is being sold, generate continuous interest and excitement in what is being sold, and finalize a sale before a competitor takes it away.

Don't sell yourself short.

NOT ENOUGH CAPITAL.

Too many new business owners underestimate how much money they need. Not to get their business off the ground, but to keep it running through the first year of operations when money is tight. That's not to say that buckets of money are needed to succeed as an entrepreneur. For example, an entrepreneur in the USA made a tidy profit writing and selling a small booklet that contained recipes for 100 different meals made with ground beef. Another American entrepreneur sold fishing lures by doing nothing more than advertising in a sports journal. For one dollar and the cost of postage, readers were asked to send in an unlucky lure for which they would receive a different lure in reply. The scheme was nothing more than a used product swap yet no one complained and it produced a small profit (Halloran, 1992).

Unfortunately, most businesses need more than a few recipes or a fishing lure to get started. You may recall that the first chapter of this book claims that passion and commitment are more important than money when it comes to starting a business. According to many practitioners, this is true, however, it's also true that most businesses don't make any money during their first year or two of operations. Funding is therefore needed to cover taxes, wages, raw materials and other costs, as well as the personal requirements of the owner (e.g. food, medical insurance, a mortgage (or rent), car expenses, and so on). With this in mind, many successful entrepreneurs suggest pursuing several sources of finance rather than just one (which could dry up). If possible, they also suggest trying to collect an additional three to six months worth of extra working capital to put aside for emergencies. If your business idea needs a lot of money to get started then you're probably thinking too big, consider starting smaller.

PRICING PROBLEMS

The price of a product is usually the most significant factor affecting a customer's decision as to whether or not the product will be bought. Entrepreneurs want to make as much money as they can while customers want to save as much money as possible. Unfortunately, it's the entrepreneur that usually loses this struggle. In a bid to attract customers, the most common pricing mistake made by new businesses (especially service providers) is to undercharge or give away labor or materials to attract customers. Yet once a product has been dispensed for free the business no longer has any leverage to collect payment.

Another factor that must be considered when establishing a good price is the amount of time, work, and effort invested in the product or service. Setting a price involves much more than covering expenses or charging what everyone else is charging.

LACK OF A COMPETITIVE EDGE

Many small businesses start as a cutout copy of another business, thereby providing no incentive for customers to choose it over the available competition. Every enterprise should therefore, have at least one aspect that distinguishes it from its competitors.

GOING AT IT ALONE

Along with not doing enough research and not establishing a close relationship with customers (as well as suppliers), going at it alone means relying totally on your own, infallible, all-knowing and superior intellect. Putting it another way, there are so many qualified people, books, education centers, and government programs that are available to help entrepreneurs that it doesn't make sense to venture into the marketplace alone. If help is needed it should be asked for.

CHAPTER NINE

CHOOSE A BUSINESS STRUCTURE

We choose our joys and sorrows long before we experience them. - Kahlil Gibran

O f all the decisions you make when starting a business, probably the most important one relating to taxes is the type of legal structure you select for your company. Not only will this decision have an impact on how much you pay in taxes, but it will affect the amount of paperwork your business is required to do, the personal liability you face and your ability to raise money.

The most common forms of business are sole proprietorship, partnership, corporation and S corporation. A more recent development to these forms of business is the limited liability company (LLC) and the limited liability partnership (LLP). Because each business form comes with different tax consequences, you will want to make your selection wisely and choose the structure that most closely matches your business's needs.

If you decide to start your business as a sole proprietorship but later decide to take on partners, you can reorganize as a partnership or other entity. If you do this, be sure you notify the IRS as well as your state tax agency.

If you operate as a sole proprietor, be sure you keep your business income and records separate from your personal finances. It helps to establish a business checking account and get a credit card to use only for business expenses.

SOLE PROPRIETORSHIP

The simplest structure is the sole proprietorship, which usually involves just one individual who owns and operates the enterprise. If you intend to work alone, this structure may be the way to go. The tax aspects of a sole proprietorship are appealing because the expenses and your income from the business are included on your personal income tax return. With a sole proprietorship, your business earnings are taxed only once, unlike other business structures. Another big plus is that you will have complete control over your business you make all the decisions.

There are a few disadvantages to consider, however. Selecting the sole proprietorship business structure means you are personally responsible for your company's liabilities. As a result, you are placing your assets at risk, and they could be seized to satisfy a business debt or a legal claim filed against you.

Raising money for a sole proprietorship can also be difficult. Banks and other financing sources may be reluctant to make business loans to sole proprietorships. In most cases, you will have to depend on your financing sources, such as savings, home equity or family loans.

PARTNERSHIP

If your business will be owned and operated by several individuals, you'll want to take a look at structuring your business as a partnership. Partnerships come in two varieties: general partnerships and limited partnerships. In a general partnership, the partners manage the company and assume responsibility for the partnership's debts and other obligations. A limited partnership has both general and limited partners. The general partners own and operate the business and assume liability for the partnership, while the limited partners serve as investors only; they have no control over the company and are not subject to the same liabilities as of the general partners.

Unless you expect to have many passive investors, limited partnerships are generally not the best choice for a new business because of all the required filings and administrative complexities. If you have two or more partners who want to be actively involved, a general partnership would be much easier to form. One of the major advantages of a partnership is the tax treatment it enjoys. A partnership does not pay tax on its income but "passes through" any profits or losses to the individual partners. At tax time, the partnership must file a tax return (Form 1065) that reports its income and loss to the IRS.

Personal liability is a major concern if you use a general partnership to structure your business. Like sole proprietors, general partners are personally liable for the partnership's obligations and debts. Each general partner can act on behalf of the partnership, take out loans and make decisions that will affect and be binding on all the partners (if the partnership agreement permits). Keep in mind that partnerships are also more expensive to establish than sole proprietorships because they require more legal and accounting services.

If you decide to organize your business as a partnership, be sure you draft a partnership agreement that details how business decisions are made, how disputes are resolved, and how to handle a buyout. You'll be glad you have this agreement if for some reason you run into difficulties with one of the partners or if someone wants out of the arrangement. The agreement should address the purpose of the business and the authority and responsibility of each partner. It's a good idea to consult an attorney experienced with small businesses for help in drafting the agreement.

CORPORATION

The corporate structure is more complex and expensive than most other business structures. A corporation is an independent legal entity, separate from its owners, and as such, it requires complying with more regulations and tax requirements. The biggest benefit for a business owner who decides to incorporate is the liability protection he or she receives. A corporation's debt is not considered that of its owners, so if you organize your business as a corporation, you are not putting your assets at risk. A corporation also can retain some of its profits without the owner paying tax on them. Another plus is the ability of a corporation to raise money. A corporation can sell a stock, either common or preferred, to raise funds. Corporations also continue indefinitely, even if one of the shareholders dies, sells the shares or becomes disabled. The corporate structure, however, comes with several downsides. A major one is higher costs. Corporations are formed under the laws of each state with its own set of regulations. You will probably need the assistance of an attorney to guide you. Also, because a corporation must follow more complex rules and regulations than a partnership or sole proprietorship, it requires more accounting and tax preparation services. Another drawback is that it requires the owners of the corporation to pay a double tax on the business's earnings. Not only are corporations subject to corporate income tax at both the federal and state levels, but any earnings distributed to shareholders in the form of dividends are taxed at individual tax rates on their income tax returns.

One strategy to help soften the blow of double taxation is to pay some money out as salary to you and any other corporate shareholders who work for the company. A corporation is not required to pay tax on earnings paid as reasonable compensation, and it can deduct the payments as a business expense. However, the IRS has limits on what it believes to be reasonable compensation.

S CORPORATION

The S corporation is more attractive to small-business owners than a regular (or C) corporation. That's because an S corporation has some appealing tax benefits and still provides business owners with the liability protection of a corporation. With an S corporation, income and losses are passed through to shareholders and included on their tax returns. As a result, there's just one level of federal tax to pay. Besides, owners of S corporations who don't have inventory can use the cash method of accounting, which is simpler than the accrual method. Under this method, income is taxable when received and expenses are deductible when paid.

S corporations can also have up to 100 shareholders. This makes it possible to have more investors and thus attract more capital, tax experts maintain. S corporations do come with some downsides. For example, S corporations are subject to many of the same rules corporations must follow, and that means higher legal and tax service costs. They also must file articles of incorporation, hold directors and shareholders meetings, keep corporate minutes, and allow shareholders to vote on major corporate decisions. The legal and accounting costs of setting up an S corporation are also similar to those for a regular corporation.

Another major difference between a regular corporation and an S corporation is that S corporations can only issue one class of stock. Experts say this can hamper the company's ability to raise capital. In addition, unlike in a regular corporation, S corporation stock can only be owned by individuals, estates and certain types of trusts.

INCORPORATING (inc.)

To start the process of incorporating, contact the secretary of state or the state office that is responsible for registering corporations in your state. Ask for instructions, forms and fee schedules on incorporating. It is possible to file for incorporation without the help of an attorney by using books and software to guide you. Your expense will be the cost of these resources, the filing fees and other costs associated with incorporating in your state. If you do it yourself, you will save the expense of using a lawyer, which can cost from $500 to $5,000 if you choose a firm that specializes in startup businesses. The disadvantage is that the process may take you some time to accomplish. There is also a chance you could miss some small but important detail in your state's law.

One of the first steps in the incorporation process is to prepare a certificate or articles of incorporation. Some states provide a printed form for this, which either you or your attorney can complete. The information requested includes the proposed name of the corporation, the purpose of the corporation, the names and addresses of those incorporating, and the location of the principal office of the corporation. The corporation will also need a set of bylaws that describe in greater detail than the articles how the corporation will run, including the responsibilities of the company's shareholders, directors and officers; when stockholder meetings will be held; and other details important to running the company. Once your articles of incorporation are accepted, the secretary of state's office will send you a certificate of incorporation.

RULES OF THE ROAD
Once you are incorporated, be sure to follow the rules of incorporation. If you fail to do so, a court can pierce the corporate veil and hold you and the other business owners personally liable for the business's debts.

It is important to follow all the rules required by state law. You should keep accurate financial records for the corporation, showing a separation between the corporation's income and expenses and those of the owners. The corporation should also issue stock, file annual reports and hold yearly meetings to elect company officers and directors, even if they're the same people as the shareholders. Be sure to keep minutes of shareholders' and directors' meetings. *On all references to your business, make certain to identify it as a corporation, using Inc. or Corp., whichever your state requires.* You also want to make sure that whomever you will be dealing with, such as your banker or clients, knows that you are an officer of a corporation.

LIMITED LIABILITY COMPANY
Limited liability companies, often referred to as "LLCs," have been around since 1977, but their popularity among entrepreneurs is a relatively recent phenomenon. An LLC is a hybrid entity, bringing together some of the best features of partnerships and corporations. LLCs were created to provide business owners with the liability protection that corporations enjoy without double taxation.

Earnings and losses pass through to the owners and are included on their personal tax returns. it sounds similar to an S corporation doesn't it? That's because it is, except that an LLC offers business owners even more attractions than an S corporation. For example, there is no limitation on the number of shareholders an LLC can have, unlike an S corporation, which has a limit of 100 shareholders. In addition, any member or owner of the LLC is allowed a full participatory role in the business's operation; in a limited partnership, on the other hand, partners are not permitted any say in the operation.

To set up an LLC, you must file articles of organization with the secretary of state in the state where you intend to do business. Some states also require you to file an operating agreement, which is similar to a partnership agreement. Like partnerships, LLCs do not have perpetual life. Some state statutes stipulate

51

that the company must dissolve after 30 years. Technically, the company dissolves when a member dies, quits or retires.

If you plan to operate in several states, you must determine how a state will treat an LLC formed in another state. If you decide on an LLC structure, be sure to use the services of an experienced accountant who is familiar with the various rules and regulations of LLCs. Another recent development is the limited liability partnership (LLP). With an LLP, the general partners have limited liability. For example, the partners are liable for their malpractice and not that of their partners. This legal form works well for those involved in professional practice, such as physicians.

THE NONPROFIT OPTION

What about organizing your venture as a nonprofit corporation? Unlike a for-profit business, a nonprofit may be eligible for certain benefits, such as sales, property and income tax exemptions at the state level. The IRS points out that while most federal tax-exempt organizations are nonprofit organizations, organizing as a nonprofit at the state level does not automatically exempt you from federal income tax.

Another major difference between profit and nonprofit business deals with the treatment of the profits. With a for-profit business, the owners and shareholders generally receive the profits. With a nonprofit, any money that is left after the organization has paid its bills is put back into the organization. Some types of nonprofits can receive contributions that are tax-deductible to the individual who contributes to the organization. Keep in mind that nonprofits are organized to provide some benefit to the public. Nonprofits are incorporated under the laws of the state in which they are established.

Remember, nonprofits still have to pay employment taxes, but in some states, they may be exempt from paying sales tax. Check with your state to make sure you understand how nonprofit status is treated in your area. Also, nonprofits may be hit with unrelated business income tax. This is regular income from a trade or business that is not substantially related to the charitable purpose.

Even after you settle on a business structure, remember that the circumstances that make one type of business organization favorable are always subject to changes in the laws. It makes sense to reassess your form of business from time to time to make sure you are using the one that provides the most benefits.

CHAPTER TEN

A WINNING BUSINESS PLAN

T ell friends you're starting a business, and you will get as many different pieces of advice as you have friends. One piece of wisdom, however, transcends all others: ***Write a business plan.***
Some people think you don't need a business plan unless you're trying to borrow money. Of course, you do indeed need a good plan if you intend to approach a lender whether a banker, a venture capitalist or any number of other sources for startup capital. But a business plan is more than a pitch for financing; it's a guide to help you define and meet your business goals. Just as you wouldn't start on a cross-country drive without a road map, you should not embark on your new business without a business plan to guide you.

A business plan won't automatically make you a success, but it will help you avoid some common causes of business failure, such as undercapitalization or lack of an adequate market. As you research and prepare your business plan, you'll find weak spots in your business idea that you'll be able to repair. You'll also discover areas with potential you may not have thought about before and ways to profit from them. Only by putting together a business plan, you then will be able to decide whether your great idea is worth your time and investment.

What is a business plan, and how do you put one together? Simply stated, a business plan conveys your business goals and the strategies you'll use to meet them, potential problems that may confront your business and ways to solve them, the organizational structure of your business (including titles and responsibilities), and the amount of capital required to finance your venture and keep it going until it breaks even. Sound impressive? It can be if put together properly. A good business plan follows generally accepted guidelines for both form and content.

There are three primary parts of a business plan.

The first is the **business concept**, where you discuss the industry, your business structure, your product or service, and how you plan to make your business a success.

The second is the **marketplace section**, in which you describe and analyze potential customers: who and where they are, what makes them buy and so on. Here, you also describe the competition and how you will position yourself to beat it.

Finally, **the financial section** contains your income and cash flow statements, balance sheet and other financial ratios, such as break-even analyses. This part may require help from your accountant and a good spreadsheet software program.

Breaking these three major sections down further, a business plan consists of seven major components:

1. Executive summary
2. Business description
3. Market strategies
4. Competitive analysis
5. Design and development plan
6. Operations and management plan
7. Financial factors

In addition to these sections, a business plan should also have a cover, title page and table of contents.

EXECUTIVE SUMMARY

Anyone looking at your business plan will first want to know what kind of business you are starting. So the business concept section should start with an executive summary, which outlines and describes the product or service you will sell.

The executive summary is the first thing the reader sees. Therefore, it must make an immediate impact by clearly stating the nature of the business and, if you are seeking capital, the type of financing you want. The executive summary describes the business, its legal form of operation (sole proprietorship, partnership, corporation or Limited Liability Company), the amount and purpose of the loan requested, the repayment schedule, the borrower's equity share, and the debt-to-equity ratio after the loan, security or collateral is offered.

Also listed are the market value, estimated value or price quotes for any equipment you plan to purchase with the loan proceeds. Your executive summary should be short and business-like generally between half a page and one page, depending on how complicated the use of funds is.

Although it's the first part of the plan to be read, the executive summary is most effective if it's the last part you write. By waiting until you have finished the rest of your business plan, you ensure you have all the relevant information in front of you. This allows you to create an executive summary that hits all the crucial points of your plan.

BUSINESS DESCRIPTION

This section expands on the executive summary, describing your business in much greater detail. It usually starts with a description of your industry. Is the business retail, wholesale, food service, manufacturing or service-oriented? How big is the industry? Why has it become so popular? What kind of trends is responsible for the industry's growth? Prove, with statistics and anecdotal information, how much opportunity there is in the industry.

Explain the target market for your product or service, how the product will be distributed, and the business' support systems that are, its advertising, promotions and customer service strategies. Next, describe your product or service. Discuss the product's applications and end-users. Emphasize any unique features or variations that set your product or service apart from others in your industry.

MARKET STRATEGIES

Here's where you define your market its size, structure, growth prospects, trends and sales potential. Based on research, interviews and sales analysis, the marketplace section should focus on your customers and your competition. How much of the market will your product or service be able to capture?

The answer is tricky since so many variables influence it. Think of it as a combination of words and numbers. Write down the who, what, when, where and why of your customers. The answer is critical to determining how you will develop pricing strategies and distribution channels. Be sure to document how and from what sources you compiled your market information. Describe how your business fits into the overall market picture. Emphasize your unique selling proposition (USP) in other words, what makes you different? Explain why your approach is ideal for your market.

Once you've clearly defined your market and established your sales goals, present the strategies you'll use to meet those goals.

Price. Thoroughly explain your pricing strategy and how it will affect the success of your product or service. Describe your projected costs and then determine the pricing based on the profit percentage you expect. Costs include materials, distribution, advertising and overhead. Many experts recommend adding 25 to 50 per cent to each cost estimate, especially overhead, to ensure you don't underestimate.

Distribution. This includes the entire process of moving the product from the factory to the end-user. The type of distribution network you choose depends on your industry and the size of the market. How much will it cost to reach your target market? Does that market consist of upscale customers who

56

will pay extra for a premium product or service, or budget-conscious consumers looking for a good deal? Study your competitors to see what channels they use. Will you use the same channels or a different method that may give you a strategic advantage?

Sales. Explain how your sales force (if you have one) will meet its goals, including elements such as pricing flexibility, sales presentations, lead generation and compensation policies.

COMPETITIVE ANALYSIS

How does your business relate to the competition? The competitive analysis section answers this question. Using what you've learned from your market research, detail the strengths and weaknesses of your competitors, the strategies that give you a distinct advantage, any barriers you can develop to prevent new competition from entering the market and any weaknesses in your competitors' service or product development cycle that you can take advantage of.

The competitive analysis is an important part of your business plan. Often, startup entrepreneurs mistakenly believe their product or service is the first of its kind and fail to recognize that competition exists. In reality, every business has competition, whether direct or indirect. Your plan must show that you recognize this and have a strategy for dealing with the competition.

Looking for inspiration? Visit the SBA (sbaonline.sba.gov/starting_business /planning/basic.html) offers clear, concise business plan outlines and tutorials. When completed, if you feel like your business plan has the right stuff, consider submitting it to a business plan competition. Universities, such as Wharton and Harvard Business School, and corporations often sponsor such competitions, offering grants and other cash prizes that can help offset your startup costs. To find a competition, Google "business plan competition" and see what turns up.

DESIGN AND DEVELOPMENT PLAN

This section describes a product's design and charts its development within the context of not yet developed product or service, if you plan to improve an existing product or service, or if you own an existing company and plan to introduce a new product or service, this section is extremely important. (If your product is already completely designed and developed, you don't need to complete this section. If you are offering a service, you will need to concentrate only on the development half of the section.)

The design section should thoroughly describe the product's design and the materials used; include any diagrams if applicable. The development plan generally covers these three areas: 1) product development, 2) market development and 3) organizational development. If you're offering a service, cover only the last two. Create a schedule that shows how the product, marketing strategies and organization will develop over time. The schedule should be tied to a development budget so expenses can be tracked throughout the design and development process.

OPERATIONS AND MANAGEMENT PLAN

Here, you describe how your business will function daily. This section explains logistics such as the responsibilities of each member of the management team, the tasks assigned to each division of the company (if applicable), and the capital and expense requirements for operating the business.

Describe the business's managers and their qualifications, and specify what type of support staff will be needed for the business to run efficiently. Any potential benefits or pitfalls to the community should also be presented, such as new job creation, economic growth, and possible effects on the environment from manufacturing and how they will be handled to conform with local, state and federal regulations.

FINANCIAL FACTORS

The financial statements are the backbone of your business plan. They show how profitable your business will be in the short and long term, and should include the following:

The income statement details the business's cash-generating ability. It projects such items as revenue, expenses, capital (in the form of depreciation) and cost of goods. You should generate a monthly income statement for the business's first year, quarterly statements for the second year and annual statements for each year thereafter (usually for three, five or ten years, with five being the most common).

The cash-flow statement details the amount of money coming into and going out of the business monthly for the first year and quarterly for each year thereafter. The result is a profit or loss at the end of the period represented by each column. Both profits and losses carry over to the last column to show a cumulative amount. If your cash-flow statement shows you consistently operating at a loss, you will probably need additional cash to meet expenses. Most businesses have some seasonal variations in their budgets, so re-examine your cash-flow calculations if they look identical every month.

The balance sheet paints a picture of the business's financial strength in terms of assets, liabilities and equity over a set period. You should generate a balance sheet for each year profiled in the development of your business.

After these essential financial documents, including any relevant summary information that's not included elsewhere in the plan but will significantly affect the business. This could include ratios such as return on investment, break-even point or return on assets. Your accountant can help you decide what information is best to include.

Many people consider the financial section of a business plan the most difficult to write. If you haven't started your business yet, how do you know what your income will be? You have a few options. The first is to enlist your accountant's help. An accountant can take your raw data and organize it into categories that will satisfy all the requirements of a financial section, including monthly and yearly sales projections. Or, if you are familiar with accounting procedures, you can do it yourself with the help of a good spreadsheet program.

OBTAINING FUNDINGS

One of the primary purposes of a business plan is to help you obtain financing for your business. When writing your plan, it's important to remember who those financing sources are likely to be. Bankers, investors, venture capitalists and investment advisors are sophisticated in business and financial matters. How can you ensure your plan makes the right impression?

These three tips are key:

Avoid hype. As an entrepreneur you don't want to gamble by relying on your gut feelings, of financial types is likely to go "by the book." If your business plan praises your idea with superlatives like "one of a kind," "unique" or "unprecedented," your readers are likely to be turned off. Wild, unsubstantiated promises or unfounded conclusions tell financial sources you are inexperienced, naive and reckless.

Polish the executive summary. Potential investors receive so many business plans, they cannot afford to spend more than a few minutes evaluating each one. If at first glance your proposal looks dull, poorly written or confusing, investors will toss it aside without a second thought. In other words, if your executive summary doesn't grab them, you won't get a second chance.

Make sure your plan is complete. Even if your executive summary sparkles, you need to make sure the rest of your plan is just as good and that all the necessary information is included. Some entrepreneurs are in such a hurry to get financing, they submit a condensed or preliminary business plan, promising to provide more information if the recipient is interested. This approach usually backfires for two reasons: First, if you don't provide information upfront, investors will assume the information doesn't exist yet and that you are stalling for time. Second, even if investors are interested in your preliminary plan, their interest may cool in the time it takes you to compile the rest of the information.

When presenting a business plan, you are starting from a position of weakness. And if potential investors find any flaws in your plan, they gain an even greater bargaining advantage. A well-written and complete plan gives you greater negotiating power and boosts your chances of getting financing on your terms.

59

SECTION THREE
WHAT NEXT….

You've put a lot of time and effort into your business plan. What happens when it's finished? A good business plan should not gather dust in a drawer. Think of it as a living document, and refer to it often. A well-written plan will help you define activities and responsibilities within your business as well as identify and achieve your goals.

To ensure your business plan continues to serve you well, make it a habit to update yours annually. Set aside a block of time near the beginning of the calendar year, fiscal year or whenever is convenient for you. Meet with your accountant or financial advisor, if necessary, to go over and update financial figures. Is your business heading in the right direction or has it wandered off course?

Making it a practice to review your business plan annually is a great way to start the year fresh and reinvigorated. It lets you catch any problems before they become too large to solve. It also ensures that if the possibility of getting financing, participating in a joint venture or other such occasion arises, you'll have an updated plan ready to go so you don't miss out on a good opportunity.

Whether you're writing it for the first time or updating it for the fifteenth, creating a good business plan doesn't mean penning a 200-page novel or adding lots of fancy clip art and footnotes. It means proving to yourself and others that you understand your business and that you know what's required to make it grow and prosper.

CHAPTER ELEVEN

HIRING PROFESSIONALS

As you start on your business journey, there are two professionals you will soon come to rely on to guide you along the path: your lawyer and your accountant. It's hard to navigate the maze of tax and legal issues facing entrepreneurs these days unless these professionals are an integral part of your team.

HIRING A LAWYER

When do you need a lawyer? Although the answer depends on your business and your particular circumstances, it's generally worthwhile to consult one before making any decision that could have legal ramifications. These include setting up a partnership or corporation, checking for compliance with regulations, negotiating loans, obtaining trademarks or patents, preparing to buy and sell agreements, assisting with tax planning, drawing up pension plans, reviewing business forms, negotiating and drawing up documents to buy or sell real estate, reviewing employee contracts, exporting or selling products in other states, and collecting bad debts. If something goes wrong, you may need an attorney to stand up for your trademark rights, go to court on an employee dispute or defend you in a product liability lawsuit. Do not wait until something goes wrong to consult an attorney, it may not be the best idea in today's litigious society. Better to start on the right foot from the beginning by doing the proper research and choosing a good lawyer. Many entrepreneurs say their relationship with a lawyer is like a marriage, it takes time to develop. That's why it's important to lay the groundwork for a good partnership early.

You can choose the right attorney by asking for recommendations from business owners in your industries or professionals such as bankers or accountants you trust. Don't just get names; ask them for the specific strengths and weaknesses of the attorneys they recommend. Next, set up an interview with the top five attorneys you're considering. Tell them you're interested in building a long-term relationship and find out which ones are willing to meet with you for an initial consultation without charging a fee. At this initial conference, be ready to describe your business and it's legal needs.

Take note of what the attorney says and does, and look for the following qualities:

Experience. Although it's not essential to find an expert in your particular field, it makes sense to look for someone who specializes in small-business problems as opposed to, say, maritime law. Find someone who understands the different business structures and their tax implications. Make sure the lawyer is willing to take on small problems; if you're trying to collect on a small invoice, will the lawyer think it's worth his or her time?

Understanding. Be sure the attorney is willing to learn about your business's goals. You're looking for someone who will be a long-term partner in your business's growth. Sure, you're a startup today, but does the lawyer understand where you want to be tomorrow and share your vision for the future?

Ability to communicate. If the lawyer speaks in legalese and doesn't bother to explain the terms he or she uses, you should look for someone else.

Availability. Will the attorney be available for conferences at your convenience, not his or hers? How quickly can you expect emergency phone calls to be returned?

Rapport. Is this someone you can get along with? You'll be discussing matters close to your heart, so make sure you feel comfortable doing so. Good chemistry will ensure a better relationship and more positive results for your business.

Reasonable fees. Attorneys charge anywhere from $50 to $1,000 or more per hour, depending on the location, size and prestige of the firm as well as the lawyer's reputation and experience. Shop around and get quotes from several firms before making your decision. However, beware of comparing one attorney with another based on fees alone. The lowest hourly fees may not indicate the best value in legal work because an inexperienced attorney may take twice as long to complete a project as an experienced one will.

References. Don't be afraid to ask for references. Ask what types of businesses or cases the attorney has worked within the past. Get a list of clients or other attorneys you can contact to discuss competence, service and fees.

When you hire an attorney, draw up an agreement (called an "engagement letter") detailing the billing method. If more than one attorney works on your file, make sure you specify the hourly rate for each individual so you aren't charged $200 an hour for legal work done by an associate who only charges $75 an hour.

This agreement should also specify what expenses you're expected to reimburse. Some attorneys expect to be reimbursed for meals, secretarial overtime, postage and photocopies, which many people consider the costs of doing business. If an unexpected charge comes up, will your attorney call you for authorization?

Agree to reimburse only reasonable and necessary out-of-pocket expenses. No matter what methods your attorney uses, here are steps you can take to control legal costs:

Have the attorney estimate the cost of each matter in writing, so you can decide whether it's worth pursuing.

Learn what increments of time the firm uses to calculate its bill.

Request monthly, itemized bills.

See if you can negotiate prompt-payment discounts.

Be prepared. Before you meet with or call your lawyer, have the necessary documents with you and know exactly what you want to discuss.

Meet with your lawyer regularly.

When you're hit with a lawsuit, the costs can be mind-boggling even if you win. That's why more and more small businesses are using alternative dispute resolution (ADR), a concept that includes mediation, arbitration and other ways of resolving disputes without resorting to litigation. Both in contracts between businesses or agreements between employers and employees, people are consenting ahead of time to submit future disputes to ADR.

Like any competent professional, a good lawyer also returns phone calls promptly, meets deadlines and follows through on promises. A good lawyer is thorough in asking for information and discerning your goals. And good lawyers either research what they do not know and explain your options, or refer you to someone who can help.

In evaluating the attorney's work on any matter, consider whether you have been able to meet your goals. If you have met your goals without undue costs, the attorney is probably doing a good job. Once you have found a lawyer who understands your business and does a good job, you have found a valuable asset.

HIRING AN ACCOUNTANT

Don't assume only big companies need the services of an accountant. Accountants help you keep an eye on major costs as early as the startup stage, a time when you're probably preoccupied with counting every paper clip and postage stamp. Accountants help you look at the big picture.

Even after the startup stage, many business owners may not have any idea how well they're doing financially until the end of the year when they file their tax returns. Meanwhile, they equate their cash flow with profits, which is wrong. Every dollar counts for business owners, so if you don't know where you stand every month, you may not be around at the end of the year.

While do-it-yourself accounting software is plentiful and easy to use, it's not the sole answer. Just as having Microsoft Word does not make you a writer, having accounting software doesn't make you an accountant. The software can only do what you tell it to do and a good accountant's skills go far beyond crunching numbers.

While many people think of accountants strictly as tax preparers, in reality, accountants have a wide knowledge base that can be an invaluable asset to a business. General accounting practice covers four basic areas of expertise:

Business advisory services

Accounting and record-keeping

Tax advice

Auditing

These four disciplines often overlap. For instance, if your accountant is helping you prepare the financial statements you need for a loan, and he or she gives you some insights into how certain estimates could be recalculated to get a more favorable review, the accountant is crossing the line from auditing into business advisory services. And perhaps, after preparing your midyear financial statements, he or she might suggest how your performance year-to-date will influence your year-end tax liability.

The best way to find a good accountant is to get a referral from your attorney, your banker or a business colleague in the same industry. If you need more possibilities, almost every state has a Society of Certified Public Accountants that will make a referral. Don't underestimate the importance of a CPA (certified public accountant). This title is only awarded to people who have passed a rigorous two-day, nationally standardized test. Most states require CPAs to have at least a college degree or its equivalent, and several states also require post-graduate work.

BUILDING OTHER RELATIONSHIPS

Mentors can be valuable sources of information at any stage of your company's growth. It is always in your best interest to reach out to a variety of sources of information when you make decisions. Mentors can often give you a fresh perspective on problems or challenges because they're not personally involved with your business like other advisors, including attorneys, accountants and friends. For this reason, it's important to find not only a mentor who has experience and knowledgeable, but also someone you can trust and feel at ease with.

Building a relationship takes work on your part, too. Everyone likes recognition, to get a note, to have someone say thank you. You get goosebumps just thinking about it. That's better than anything for a mentor.

Other mentoring resources can be found through networking in your community. Attend luncheons, seminars, and conferences related to your business and talk to guest speakers. Find out what types of business organizations closely match your company so you can team up with other individuals with similar interests and concerns. Developing these types of personal and business relationships can put you in touch with successful people who may be potential mentors.

CHAPTER TWELVE

GETTING FUNDS

O nce you have decided on the type of venture you want to start, the next step on the road to business success is figuring out where the money will come from to fund it. Where do you start? The best place to begin is by looking in the mirror. Self-financing is the number-one form of financing used by most business startups. Also, when you approach other financing sources such as bankers, venture capitalists or the government, they will want to know exactly how much of your own money you are putting into the venture. You must have enough faith in your business to risk your own money.

PERSONAL INVENTORY

Begin by doing a thorough inventory of your assets. You are likely to uncover resources you didn't even know you had. Assets include savings accounts, equity in real estate, retirement accounts, vehicles, recreational equipment and collections. You may decide to sell some assets for cash or to use them as collateral for a loan.

If you have investments, you may be able to use them as a resource. Low-interest margin loans against stocks and securities can be arranged through your brokerage accounts. The downside here is that if the market should fall and your securities are your loan collateral, you'll get a margin call from your broker, requesting you to supply more collateral. If you can't do that within a certain time, you'll be asked to sell some of your securities to shore up the collateral. Also, take a look at your personal line of credit. Some businesses have successfully been started on credit cards, although this is one of the most expensive ways to finance yourself. If you own a home, consider getting a home equity loan on the part of the mortgage that you have already paid off. The bank will either provide a lump-sum loan payment or extend a line of credit based on the equity in your home. Depending on the value of your home, a home equity loan could become a substantial line of credit. Consider borrowing against cash-value life insurance. You can use the value built up in a cash-value life insurance policy as a ready source of cash. The interest rates are reasonable because the insurance companies always get their money back. You don't even have to make payments if you do not want to. Neither the amount you borrow nor the interest that accrues, has to be repaid. The only loss is that if you die and the debt hasn't been repaid, that money is deducted from the amount your beneficiary will receive.

If you have a retirement plan through your employer and are starting a part-time business while you keep your full-time job, consider borrowing against the plan. It's very common for such plans to allow you to borrow up to 50 per cent of your vested account balance. The interest rate is usually 1 to 2 per cent above the prime rate with a specified repayment schedule. The downside of borrowing from your retirement plan is that if you lose your job, the loan has to be repaid in a short period. Consult the plan's documentation to see if this is an option for you.

If you are employed, another way to finance your business is by squirreling away money from your current salary until you have enough to launch the business. If you don't want to wait, consider moonlighting or cutting your full-time job back to part-time. This ensures you'll have some steady funds rolling in until your business starts to soar.

People generally have more assets than they realize. Use as much of your own money as possible to get started; remember, the larger your own investment, the easier it will be for you to acquire capital from other sources.

FRIENDS AND FAMILY

Your own resources may not be enough to give you the capital you need. "Most businesses are started with money from four or five different sources. After self-financing, the second most popular source for startup money is composed of friends, relatives and business associates.

These people know you have integrity and will grant you a loan based on the strength of your character. It makes sense. People with whom you have close relationships know you are reliable and competent, so there should be no problem in asking for a loan, right? Keep in mind, however, that asking for financial help isn't the same as borrowing the car. While squeezing money out of family and friends may seem an easy alternative to dealing with bankers, it can be a much more delicate situation.

Once you determine whom you'd like to borrow money from, approach the person initially in an informal situation. Let the person know a little about your business, and gauge his or her interest. If the person seems interested and says he or she would like more information about the business, make an appointment to meet with them in a professional atmosphere. "This makes it clear that the subject of discussion will be your business and their interest in it, "You may secure their initial interest in a casual setting, but to go beyond that, you have to make an extra effort. You should do a formal sales presentation and make sure the person has all the facts. Be prepared to accept rejection gracefully. Don't pile on the emotional pressure, emphasize that you'd like this to be strictly a business decision for them. If relatives or friends feel they can turn you down without offending you, they're more likely to invest. Give them an out.

Ensure that you state how much you need, what you'll use it for, and a plan on how you'll pay it back. Next, draw up the legal papers an agreement stating that the person will indeed put money into the business. Make sure your agreement is in writing if you expect it to be binding. "Any time you take money into a business, the law is very explicit: You must have all agreements written down and documented. If you don't, emotional and legal difficulties could result in things end up in court. And if the loan isn't documented, you may find yourself with no legal recourse.

HOW TO ATTRACT INVESTORS

No matter what type of financing source you approach, a bank, a venture capitalist or your cousin. There are two basic ways to finance a business: equity financing and debt financing. In equity financing, you receive capital in exchange for part ownership of the company. In debt financing, you receive capital in the form of a loan, which must be paid back.

EQUITY BASICS

Equity financing can come from various sources, including venture capital firms and private investors. Whichever source you choose, there are some basics you should understand before you try to get equity capital. An investor's "share in your company" comes in various forms. If your company is incorporated, the investor might bargain for shares of stock. Or an investor who wants to be involved in the management of the company could come in as a partner.

Keeping control of your company can be more difficult when you are working with outside investors who provide equity financing. Before seeking outside investment, make the most of your own resources to build the company. The more value you can add before you go to the well, the better. If all you bring to the table is a good idea and some talent, an investor may not be willing to provide a large chunk of capital without receiving a controlling share of the ownership in return. As a result, you could end up losing control of the business you started. Don't assume the first investor to express interest in your business is a godsend. Even someone who seems to share your vision for the company may be bad news. It pays to know your investor. An investor who doesn't understand your business may pull the plug at the wrong time and destroy the company.

HOW DOES EQUITY WORKS

Because equity financing involves trading partial ownership interest for capital, the more capital a company takes in from equity investors, the more diluted the founder's control. The question is, how much management are you willing to give up?

Don't overlook the importance of voting control in the company. Investors may be willing to accept a majority of the preferred (nonvoting) stock rather than common (voting) stock. Another possibility is to give the investor a majority of the profits by granting dividends to the preferred stockholders first. Or, holders of nonvoting stock can get liquidation preference, meaning they're first in line to recover their investment if the company goes under.

Even if they're willing to accept a minority position, financiers generally insist on contract provisions that permit them to make management changes under certain conditions. These might include agreements permitting the investor to take control of the company if the corporation fails to meet a certain income level or makes changes without the investor's permission.

Investors may ask that their preferred stock be redeemable either for common stock or for cash a specified number of years later. That gives the entrepreneur a chance to buy the company back if possible but also may allow the investor to convert to common stock and gain control of the company. Some experts contend that retaining voting control is not important. In a typical high-growth company, the founder only owns 10 per cent of the business by the time it goes public. That's not necessarily bad, because 10 per cent of $100 million is better than 100 per cent of nothing. The key is how valuable the founder is to the success of the company. If you can't easily be replaced, then you have a lot of leverage even though you may not control the business.

If the entrepreneur is good enough, the investors may find their best alternative is to let the entrepreneur run the company. Try not to get hung up on the precise percentage of ownership: If it's a successful business, most people will leave you alone even if they own 80 per cent. To protect yourself, however, you should always seek financial and legal advice before involving outside investors in your business.

When it comes to pitching to investors, it's not what you say, but how you say it. Here's how to improve: Breath. Enunciate. Pace yourself, speaking neither too quickly nor too slowly. Nervous? Fess up admitting your insecurity puts the listeners on your side. Finally, remember practice makes perfect.

VENTURE CAPITAL

When most people think of equity financing, they think of venture capital. Once seen as a plentiful source of financing for startup businesses, venture capital like most kinds of capital is no longer so easy to come by. The ready to give venture capitalist is becoming very elusive. Yes, there are venture capital firms out there. Quite a few. There are websites you can go to, like Entrepreneur.com's (entrepreneur.com/vc100) that keeps a directory of venture capital firms. Money can be found for investing in your company, however, venture capitalist no longer hands over forklifts of money again especially for startups.

Venture capital is most likely to be given to an established company with an already proven track record. If you are a startup, your product or service must be better than sliced bread with an extremely convincing plan that will make the investor a lot of money.

THE INVESTORS ANGELS

The unpleasant reality is that getting financing from venture capital firms is an extreme long shot. The pleasant reality is that there are plenty of other sources you can tap for equity financing—typically with far fewer strings attached than an institutional venture capital deal. One source of private capital is an investment angel.

Originally a term used to describe investors in Broadway shows, "angel" now refers to anyone who invests his or her money in an entrepreneurial company (unlike institutional venture capitalists, who invest other people's money). Angel investing has soared in recent years as a growing number of individuals seek better returns on their money than they can get from traditional investment vehicles. Contrary to popular belief, most angels are not millionaires. Typically, they earn between $60,000 and $200,000 a year, which means there are likely to be plenty of them right in your backyard.

They Can Be Classified Into Two Groups; the affiliated and non-affiliated.

An affiliated angel is someone who has some sort of contact with you or your business but is not necessarily related to or acquainted with you. A non-affiliated angel has no connection with either you or your business. It is preferable to start your investor search by seeking an affiliated angel since he or she is already familiar with you or your business and has a vested interest in the relationship.

Begin by jotting down the names of people who might fit the category of an affiliated angel.

Professionals. These include professional providers of services you now use doctors, dentists, lawyers, accountants and so on. You know these people, so an appointment should be easy to arrange. Professionals usually have discretionary income available to invest in outside projects, and if they're not interested, they may be able to recommend a colleague who is.

Business associates. These are people you come in contact with during the normal course of your business day. They can be divided into four subgroups:

Suppliers/vendors. The owners of companies who supply your inventory and other needs have a vital interest in your company's success and make excellent angels. A supplier's investment may not come in the form of cash but in the form of better payment terms or cheaper prices. Suppliers might even use their credit to help you get a loan.

Customers. These are especially good contacts if they use your product or service to make or sell their goods. List all the customers with whom you have this sort of business relationship.

Employees. Some of your key employees might be sitting on unused equity in their homes that would make excellent collateral for a business loan to your business. There is no greater incentive to an employee than to share ownership in the company for which he or she works.

Competitors. These include owners of similar companies you don't directly compete with. If a competitor is doing business in another part of the country and does not infringe on your territory, he or she may be an empathetic investor and may share not only capital but information as well.

The non-affiliated angel's category includes:

Professionals. This group can include lawyers, accountants, consultants and brokers whom you don't know personally or do business with.

Middle managers. Angels in middle management positions start investing in small businesses for two major reasons either they're bored with their jobs and are looking for outside interests, or they are nearing retirement or fear they are being phased out.

Entrepreneurs. These angels are and (or have been) successful in their own businesses and like investing in other entrepreneurial ventures. Entrepreneurs who are familiar with your industry make excellent investors.

CONNECT WITH ANGELS

Approaching affiliated angels is simply a matter of calling to make an appointment. To look for non-affiliated angels, try these proven methods:

Advertising. The business opportunity section of your local newspaper or The Wall Street Journal is an excellent place to advertise for investors. Classified advertising is inexpensive, simple, quick and effective.

Business brokers. Business brokers know hundreds of people with money who are interested in buying businesses. Even though you don't want to sell your business, you might be willing to sell part of it. Since many brokers are not open to the idea of their clients buying just part of a business, you might have to use some persuasion to get the broker to give you contact names. You'll find a list of local business brokers in the Yellow Pages under "Business Brokers."

Telemarketing. This approach has been called "dialing for dollars." First, you get a list of wealthy individuals in your area. Then you begin calling them. Obviously, you have to be highly motivated to try this approach, and a good list is your most important tool. Look up mailing-list brokers in the Yellow Pages. If you don't feel comfortable making cold calls yourself, you can always hire someone to do it for you.

Networking. Attending local venture capital group meetings and other business associations to make contacts is a time-consuming approach but can be effective. Most newspapers contain an events calendar that lists when and where these types of meetings take place.

Intermediaries. These are firms that find angels for entrepreneurial companies. They are usually called "boutique investment bankers." This means they are small firms that focus primarily on small financing deals. These firms typically charge a percentage of the amount of money they raise for you. Ask your lawyer or accountant for the name of a reputable firm in your area.

Matchmaking services. Matchmakers run the gamut from services that offer face time with investors to websites that post business plans for companies seeking investments. Fundraising success often hinges on the matchmaker's screening process. In other words: Does the matchmaker have a rigorous selection process, or does it take money from anyone regardless of funding prospects? While rates vary, a matchmaking service may charge as much as $25,000 to locate investors, in addition to a percentage of funds raised. Before using any matchmaker, obtain a list of clients to assess recent successes and failures. An example of such is IdeaCrossing, which serves both the angel and venture capital communities. Its mission is to identify and screen new investment opportunities, then connect individuals with organizations to support and promote entrepreneurial activity. For more information, visit Google "investor matchmaking."

Angels tend to find most of their investment opportunities through friends and business associates, so whatever method you use to search for angels, it is also important to spread the word. Tell your professional advisors and people you meet at networking events, or anyone who could be a good source of referrals, that you are looking for investment capital. You never know what kind of people they know.

OBTAINING THE FUND

Once you've found potential angels, how do you win them over? Angels look for many of the same things professional venture capitalists look for:

Strong management. Does your management team have a track record of success and experience?

Proprietary strength. Proprietary does not necessarily mean you must have patents, copyrights or trademarks on all your products. It just means that your product or service should be unusual enough to grab consumers' attention.

The window of opportunity. Investors look for a window of opportunity when your company can be the first in a market and grab the lion's share of business before others.

Market potential. Investors prefer businesses with strong market potential. That means a restaurateur with plans to franchise stands a better chance than one who simply wants to open one local site.

Return on investment. Most angels will expect a return of 20 to 25 per cent over five years. However, they may accept a lower rate of return if your business has a lower risk.

Looking for an investor through classified ads? Be aware there are legal implications when you solicit money through the newspaper. Always get legal advice before placing an ad.

If angels consider the same factors as venture capital companies, what is the difference between them?

You have an edge with angels because many are not motivated solely by profit. Particularly if your angel is a current or former entrepreneur, he or she may be motivated as much by the enjoyment of helping a young business succeed as by the money he or she stands to gain. Angels are more likely than venture capitalists to be persuaded by an entrepreneur's drive to succeed, persistence and mental discipline. That is why your business plan must convey a good sense of your background, experience and drive. Your business plan should also address the concerns above and spell out the financing you expect to need from startup to maturity.

What if your plan is rejected? Don't take it to heart, it is part of the growth process; people say YES or NO. Ask the angel if he or she knows someone else your business might appeal to.

If your plan is accepted, you have some negotiating to do. Be sure to spell out all the terms of the investment in a written agreement; get your lawyer's assistance here.

How long will the investment last? How will the return be calculated? How will the investment be cashed out? Detail the amount of involvement each angel will have in the business and how the investment will be legalized. Examine the deal carefully for the possibility of the investor parlaying current equity or future loans to your business into controlling interest.

LASTLY INVOLVE YOUR LAWYER THROUGH THE PROCESS

DEBT FINANCING

Unlike equity financing, where you sell part of your business to an investor, debt financing simply means receiving money in the form of a loan that you will have to repay. There are many sources you can turn to for debt financing, including banks, commercial lenders and even your personal credit cards.

There is a mind-boggling variety of loans available, complicated by the fact that the same type of loan may have different terms at different banks. Here is a look at how lenders generally structure loans, with common variations.

Line-of-Credit Loans

The most useful type of loan for the small business is the line-of-credit loan. It's probably the one permanent loan arrangement every business owner should have with his or her banker since it protects the business from emergencies and stalled cash flow. Line-of-credit loans are intended for purchases of inventory and payment of operating costs for working capital and business cycle needs. They are not intended for purchases of equipment or real estate.

It is a short-term loan that extends the cash available in your business's checking account to the upper limit of the loan contract and usually carries the lowest interest rate a bank offers since they are seen as fairly low-risk. Some banks even include a clause that gives them the right to cancel the loan if they think your business is in jeopardy. Interest payments are made monthly, and the principal is paid off at your convenience. It is wise to make payments on the principal often. Bankers may also call this a revolving line of credit, and they see it as an indication that your business is earning enough income.

Most line-of-credit loans are written for periods of one year and may be renewed almost automatically for an annual fee. Some banks require that your credit line be fully paid off for seven to 30 days each contract year. This period is probably the best time to negotiate.

Even if you don't need a line-of-credit loan now, talk to your banker about how to get one. To negotiate a credit line, your banker will want to see current financial statements, the latest tax returns and a projected cash-flow statement.

You may want to apply from the comforts of home. Some varying online lenders analyze your loan application against a database of 800 commercial mortgage lenders and come up with offers from the top 30 or so lenders who want your business. It may also be a good trial run to help you determine whether you're ready to get a loan for your business.

Installment Loans

These loans are paid back with equal monthly payments covering both principal and interest. Installment loans may be written to meet all types of business needs. You receive the full amount when the contract is signed, and interest is calculated from that date to the final day of the loan. If you repay an installment loan before its final date, there will be no penalty and an appropriate adjustment of interest. The term of an installment loan will always be correlated to its use. A business cycle loan may be written as a four-month installment loan from, say, September 1 until December 31, and would carry the low-interest rate since the risk to the lender is under one year. Business cycle loans may be written from one to seven years, while real estate and renovation loans may be written for up to 21 years. An installment loan is occasionally written with quarterly, half-yearly or annual payments when monthly payments are inappropriate.

Interim Loans

When considering interim loans, bankers are concerned with who will be paying off the loan and whether that commitment is reliable. Interim loans are used to make periodic payments to the contractors building new facilities when a mortgage on the building will be used to pay off the interim loan.

Secured and Unsecured Loans

Loans can come in one of two forms: secured or unsecured. When your lender knows you well and is convinced that your business is sound and that the loan will be repaid on time, he or she may be willing to write an unsecured loan. Such a loan, in any of the aforementioned forms, has no collateral pledged as a secondary payment source should you default on the loan. The lender provides you with an unsecured loan because it considers you a low risk. As a new business, you are highly unlikely to qualify for an unsecured loan; it generally requires a track record of profitability and success.

A secured loan, on the other hand, requires some kind of collateral but generally has a lower interest rate than an unsecured loan. When a loan is written for more than 12 months, is used to purchase equipment or does not seem risk-free, the lender will ask that the loan be secured by collateral. The collateral used, whether real estate or inventory, is expected to outlast the loan and is usually related to the purpose of the loan.

Since lenders expect to use the collateral to pay off the loan if the borrower defaults, they will value it appropriately. A $20,000 piece of new equipment will probably secure a loan of up to $15,000; receivables are valued for loans up to 75 per cent of the amount due, and inventory is usually valued at up to 50 per cent of its sale price.

Letter of Credit

Typically used in international trade, this document allows entrepreneurs to guarantee payment to suppliers in other countries. The document substitutes the bank's credit for the entrepreneur up to a set amount for a specified period.

Other Loans

Banks all over the country write loans, especially installment loans, under a myriad of names. They include:

Term loans, both short- and long-term, according to the number of years they are written for.

Second mortgages where real estate is used to secure a loan; usually long-term, they're also known as equity loans.

Inventory loans and equipment loans for the purchase of, and secured by, either equipment or inventory

Accounts receivable loans secured by your outstanding accounts

Personal loans where your signature and personal collateral guarantee the loan, which you, in turn, lend to your business

Guaranteed loans in which a third party, an investor, spouse, or the SBA guarantees repayment

Commercial loans in which the bank offers its standard loan for small businesses

Once you have an understanding of the different types of loans available, you are better equipped for the next step: "selling" a lender on your business.

CHAPTER THIRTEEN

SOURCES OF FINANCING

When seeking debt financing, where do you begin? Carefully choosing the lenders you target can increase your odds of success. Here is a look at various loan sources and what you should know about each of them.

BANKS

In recent years, however, the relationship between banks and small businesses has been improving as more and more banks realize the strength and importance of this growing market. With corporations and real estate developers no longer spurring so much of banks' business, lenders are looking to entrepreneurs to take up the slack.

Many major banks have added special services and programs for small businesses; others are streamlining their loan paperwork and approval process to get loans to entrepreneurs faster. On the plus side, banks are marketing to small businesses like never before. On the downside, however, the "streamlining" process often means that, more than ever, loan approval is based solely on numbers and scores on standardized rating systems rather than on an entrepreneur's character or drive. Even given today's banking climate, it is easier to get a startup loan from community banks. They can be a little more flexible, don't have a bureaucracy to deal with, and are more apt to make character loans.

Do not get the idea that obtaining a loan from a community bank is a snap, however. You'll still have to meet credit and collateral requirements just as you would at a larger institution. The difference: Smaller banks tend to give more weight to personal attributes. If the business is located in town, the banker likely already knows the entrepreneur, and the family has lived in the area for years; these things count more in a community bank.

Whether the bank you target is big or small, perhaps what matters most is developing relationships. If you have done your personal banking at the same place for 20 years and know the people with authority there, it makes sense to target that bank as a potential lender. If you do not have that kind of relationship at your bank, start to get to know bankers now. Visit chamber of commerce meetings; go to networking events; take part in community functions that local bankers or other movers and shakers are part of. A banker with a personal interest in you is more likely to look favorably on your loan application.

Boost your chances of getting a loan by finding a lender whose experience matches your needs. Talk to friends, lawyers or accountants and other entrepreneurs in the same industry for leads on banks that have helped people in your business. Pound the pavement and talk to banks about the type and size of loans they specialize in. Put in the work to find the right lender, and you'll find it pays off.

COMMERCIAL FINANCE COMPANIES

Banks aren't your only option when seeking a loan. Nonbank commercial lenders, or commercial finance companies, have expanded their focus on small business in recent years as more and more small banks, which traditionally made loans to entrepreneurs, have been swallowed up in mergers. The advantage of approaching commercial finance companies is that, like community banks, they may be more willing to look beyond numbers and assets. Commercial finance companies give opportunities to startups and a lot of other companies banks will not lend to.

Commercial lenders require a business plan, personal financial statements and cash-flow projections and will usually expect you to come up with 20 to 25 per cent of the needed capital yourself.

FRANCHISE

Financing is any startup entrepreneur's biggest challenge, and it's no different for franchisees. The good news is, franchisors may offer a little extra help in getting the capital you need. Some franchisors offer direct financing to help franchisees with all or part of the costs of startup. This may take the form of equipment, real estate or inventory financing. The goal is to free up money so franchisees have more working capital.

Many franchisors are not directly involved in lending but have established relationships with banks and commercial finance companies. Because these lenders have processed loans for other franchisees, they are more familiar with new franchisees' needs.

CREDIT CARDS

One potentially risky way to finance your business is to use your personal credit cards. The obvious drawback is the high-interest rates; if you use the cards for cash advances rather than to buy equipment, the rates are even higher. Experts advise using credit card financing as a last resort because interest rates are higher than any other type of financing.

However, if you are good at juggling payments, your startup needs are low, and you are confident you'll be able to pay the money back fairly quickly, this could be the route to take.

"You fail if you don't try. If you try and you fail, yes, you'll have a few articles saying you've failed at something. But don't stop trying" - Richard Branson.

CHAPTER FOURTEEN

APPLYING FOR A LOAN

T he next step is applying for the loan. It's important to know what you'll need to provide and what lenders are looking for. Think of your loan application as a sales tool, just like your brochures or ads. When you put together the right combination of facts and figures, your application will sell your lender on the short and long-term profit potential of lending money to your business.

To do that, the application must convince your lender that you will pay back the loan as promised and that your managerial ability (and future loans) will result in a profit-making partnership. Banks are in the money-lending business. To lend money, they need evidence of security and stability. It's that simple. How can you provide this evidence when your business hasn't even gotten off the ground? Begin by making sure your loan application is both realistic and optimistic.

Also, make sure your application is complete. When a piece of an application is missing, bankers instantly suspect that either something is being hidden or the applicant doesn't know his or her business well enough to pull the information together.

12 separate items should be included in every loan application. The importance of each one varies with the size of your business, your industry and the amount you are requesting.

1. **Cover sheet**; this is the title page to your "book." All it needs to say is "Loan application submitted by Ben Deep, Sunday's Ice Cream Parlor, to Big Bucks Bank, Main Street, and Any town." It should also include the date and your business telephone number

2. **Cover letter**; the cover letter is a personal business letter to your banker requesting consideration of your application for a line of credit or an installment

loan. The second paragraph should describe your business: "Our Company is a sole proprietorship, partnership or corporation in manufacturing, distributing and retailing X type of goods." The third paragraph is best kept to just one or two sentences that "sell" your application by indicating what your plans are for your business.

3. **Table of contents**; this page makes it easy for your banker to see that all the documents are included.

4. **The amount and use of the loan;** this page documents how much you want to borrow and how you will use the loan. If you are buying a new piece of equipment, for instance, it should show the contract price, add the cost of freight and installation, deduct the amount you will be contributing, and show the balance to be borrowed.

5. **History and description of your business;** this is often the most difficult to write. The key is to stay with the facts and assume the reader knows nothing about your business. Describe, more fully than in the cover letter, the legal form of your business and its location. Tell why you believe the business is going to succeed. Conclude with a paragraph on your future plans.

6. **Functions and background of your management team**; Bankers know that it's people who make things happen. Your management team might consist of every employee if they oversee an important part of your operation, or it might be just you and one key person. It also includes any outside consultants you plan to use regularly, such as your accountant or banker. In one or two pages, list each person's name and responsibilities. Where appropriate, describe the background that makes this person the right choice for that job.

7. **Market information on your product or service;** you should begin these pages with a complete description of your product line or service, and the market it is directed toward. Next, describe how you have targeted your market niche and how successful you have been. Finally, detail your future plans to add new products or services.

8. **Financial history and current status**; Most bankers want to see balance sheets and income (profit and loss) statements. As a startup, you will need to use projections. Bankers will compare these to norms in your industry.

9. **Financial projections to demonstrate that the loan will be repaid;** this set of three documents a projected income statement, balance sheet and cash-flow statement should show how the business, with the use of the loan, will generate sufficient profits to pay off the loan. Your accountant can help you prepare these documents.

10. **A list of possible collateral;** listing your available collateral cash reserves, stocks and bonds, equipment, home equity, inventory and receivables demonstrates your understanding that your banker will normally look for a

backup repayment source. Each piece of collateral listed should be described with its cost and current fair market value.

11. **Personal financial statements**; as a startup, you will need to add your personal guarantee to any loan the bank makes. The banker will want to see your tax return and balance sheets showing personal net worth. Most banks have preprinted forms that make pulling these figures together relatively easy.

12. **Additional documents to support the projections**; In this section, you can include whatever documents you feel will enhance your loan package. This might include a copy of the sales contract on a new piece of equipment, a lease and photograph of a new location, blueprints or legal documents. If you are introducing a new product or service, include a product brochure and additional market research information.

THE LENDERS GUIDE TO DECISION MAKING

Your application is complete, with every "i" dotted and every "t" crossed. But is it enough to get you the cold, hard cash? What are lenders looking for when they pore over your application? Lenders typically base their decisions on four criteria, often called the "Four C's of Credit":

1. **Credit.** The lender will examine your personal credit history to see how well you've managed your past obligations. If you have some black marks on your credit, the banker will want to hear the details and see proof that you repaid what you owed. A couple of late payments are not a big deal, but two or more consecutive missed payments are. Get a copy of your credit history before you turn in your application. This way, you can find out about any problems and explain to them before your banker brings them up.

2. **Character.** Character is hard to measure, but lenders will use your credit history to assess this as well. They take lawsuits, bankruptcies and tax liens particularly seriously in evaluating your character. They will also do a background check and evaluate your previous work experience.

3. **Capacity**. What happens if your business slumps? Do you have the capacity to convert other assets to cash, either by selling or borrowing against them? Your secondary repayment sources may include real estate, stocks and other savings. The lender will look at your business balance sheet and financial statement to determine your capacity.

4. **Collateral.** As a startup, you will most likely be seeking a secured loan. This means you must put up collateral either personal assets, such as stocks or certificates of deposit, or business assets like inventory, equipment or real estate.

CHAPTER FIFTEEN

GOVERNMENT LOANS

The local, state and federal governments sometimes offer financial resources for small businesses if and when certain requirements are met. Examples include businesses that employ handicapped people (or minorities), businesses located in areas in need of economic assistance, businesses designed to help the environment, or businesses designed to reduce local problems. Contact your local economic development office for details.

The federal government has a vested interest in encouraging the growth of the small business. As a result, some Small Business Administration (SBA) loans have less stringent requirements for owner's equity and collateral compared to commercial loans, making the SBA an excellent financing source for startups. In addition, many SBA loans are for smaller sums than most banks are willing to lend. Of course, that doesn't mean the SBA is giving money away. The SBA does not make direct loans; instead, it provides loan guarantees to entrepreneurs, promising the bank to pay back a certain percentage of your loan if you are unable to.

Banks participate in the SBA program as regular, certified or preferred lenders. The SBA can help you prepare your loan package, which you then submit to banks. If the bank approves you, it submits your loan package to the SBA. Applications submitted by regular lenders are reviewed by the SBA in an average of two weeks, certified lender applications are reviewed in three days, and approval through preferred lenders is even faster.

The most basic eligibility requirement for SBA loans is the ability to repay the loan from cash flow, but the SBA also looks at personal credit history, industry experience or other evidence of management ability, collateral and owner's equity contributions.

GRANTS

When most people think of grants, they think of money given free to non-profit organizations. But profit companies, and frequently startups, can also win grant money. But how do you find these grants? Unfortunately, locating the right grant is a little like looking for your soul mate. The grant is out there, but you're going to have to do a lot of looking to find a good match.

Grants provide money that does not have to be paid back. Universities, professional organizations, governments, and trade associations are typical grant sources (including the European Union - if the business is in Europe). The unemployed, pensioners, young entrepreneurs, artists, and other out-of-the-mainstream groups are usually the most eligible to receive a grant if they qualify as competent people who are trying to set up a business in an underdeveloped area. For the most part, grants do not involve large sums of money but for a fledgling business, a small amount of cash can go a long way toward reducing expenses. Grants can also be obtained for employee training, marketing costs, and insurance. Don't be ashamed to ask for help in the form of a grant. Just be prepared to fill out lots of forms before and after any money is received.

Even in the most economically challenging times, the government is one of the best sources for grants. For instance, the National Institute of Standards and Technology's Advanced Technology Program offers grants to co-fund "high-risk, high-payoff projects" to provide Americans with a higher standard of living. Whatever the project is, you can bet it will be scrutinized by a board of qualified experts and academia.

Of course, finding the grant is the easy part; the hard part is getting the grant. It's a lot like applying to college. You have to jump through the hoops of each organization, which usually involves writing an extensive essay on why you need the money. There are grant-writing businesses out there as well as grant brokers, people who try to find the right grant for you. You pay them regardless of whether they find you a grant; on the other hand, if they land you a $750,000 grant, you still pay them the flat fee, which is generally from $25 to $100 an hour, depending on their level of success. But if you don't have the funds to pay for a grant-writer or a broker, and you're a decent writer and have a passion for your business, then start researching, and fill out the forms and compose the essay yourself. No rule says you can't try to get a grant on your own. And you might be successful!

THE TIP

A good relationship with your banker is just as important after you get that loan as it is in getting one in the first place. The keyword is "communication." The bank wants to be told all the good news and bad news about your business as soon as it occurs. Most business owners fear telling bankers bad news, but keeping problems hidden would be a mistake. Like any relationship, yours with your banker is built on trust. Keep him or her apprised of your business's progress. Invite your banker to visit your business and see how the proceeds of the loan are being put to good use.

Once you've established a relationship with a banker, it is simple to expand your circle of friends at the bank. Every time you visit, spend some time meeting and talking to people, especially those further up the ladder. Often, the bankers will be the ones to initiate contact. Take advantage of this opportunity. The more people you know at the bank, the easier it will be to get the next round of financing.

SECTION FOUR
SET FOR BUSINESS
You have a great idea, a perfect plan, and the money to make it all happen. What's the next step? First, I'll show you how to get what you want out of every deal, with negotiating tips that will put you in the driver's seat in any situation, choosing the best business location as well as creating an excellent company image which will improve your market sales.

CHAPTER SIXTEEN

THE ART OF NEGOTIATING SUCCESSFULLY

I f you're in business, you're a negotiator. You have no choice. Business doesn't happen unless two or more people enter into a transaction. This can be as simple as buying inventory or as complicated as a merger of two public companies. Without transactions, the business doesn't happen, and every transaction involves a certain amount of negotiation. The scariest challenges facing every startup entrepreneur is learning how to negotiate.

The goal in negotiating is to win, to get the best deal you can.

To be a good negotiator, you must know these three things

Your bargaining position. In every negotiation, someone is in a stronger position and someone is in a weaker position. Find a balance and strike.

How the other side perceives its position isn't enough to know what your real bargaining position is. You also have to consider how each side perceives its position.

Assess your bargaining style. You can be pleasant and communicate your willingness to get the deal done as quickly and efficiently as possible. Just make sure the other side doesn't misinterpret your nice behavior as a sign of weakness, or you'll lose the negotiation.

THE NEGOTIATION PROCESS

There are three basic steps in any negotiation sometimes they happen in order, sometimes not.

State your position. At the beginning of a negotiation, each side lays out its position and tells the other side what it needs. As soon as it's apparent the two sides agree on something, that point is taken off the table so the parties can focus on the issues where they disagree.

Search for win-win compromises. Sometimes when a negotiator asks for something, what he or she really needs is a lot narrower. By probing the other side, you can often find a way to give them what they need without giving them everything they're asking for. Here's an example: The other side wants you to promise you won't compete with them anywhere in the State of X for five years. By asking probing questions, you learn that the other side doesn't plan to do business outside of Town Y. You agree not to compete with the other side in Town Y for five years, and keep your options open for the rest of the state.

Do a little "horse-trading." Sooner or later, in every negotiation, you get to a point where further compromise is impossible. For a deal to happen at this point, both sides have to engage in a little "horse-trading." You look at the list of three open points, realizing that only one of them is a deal point, and offer to give in on the other two points to get the one you need. If the other side agrees (one or both of the two points you gave them were deal points for them), then you make the deal. If the other side refuses (your deal point was also their deal point), then the negotiation's over, and so is the deal.

EVERYTHING IS NEGOTIABLE

When you first start negotiating, it's hard to separate deal points from trading points everything seems important. Experienced negotiators know something you don't, everything is a trading point. Nothing is non-negotiable. If you need the deal badly enough, you can give up some deal points and still survive to negotiate another day. As any lawyer will tell you, you know a deal has been well-negotiated when both sides walk away from the table feeling at least somewhat disappointed in the outcome.

CHAPTER SEVENTEEN

CHOOSING A BUSINESS LOCATION

One expert will tell you location is vital to your company's success; another will argue that it doesn't matter where you are and they're both right. How important the location is for your new company depends on the type of business and the facilities and other resources you need, and where your customers are. Some version of nontraditional space may work for you, so use your imagination.

Home-based. This is probably the trendiest location for a business these days, and many entrepreneurs start at home and then move into commercial space as their business grows. Others start at home with no thought or intention of ever moving. You can run a home-based business from an office in a spare bedroom, the basement, the attic even the kitchen table. Also, you do not need to worry about negotiating leases, coming up with substantial deposits or commuting. On the downside, your room for physical growth is limited, and you may find accommodating employees or meetings with clients a challenge. Working from home makes a lot of sense when you're launching a business and have limited startup funds. In addition to saving beaucoup bucks on operating expenses like rent and utilities, you'll save on commuting costs and wardrobe expenses.

Retail. Retail space comes in a variety of shapes and sizes and may be located in free-standing buildings, enclosed malls, strip shopping centers, downtown shopping districts, or mixed-use facilities. You will also find retail space in airports and other transportation facilities, hotel lobbies, sports stadiums, and temporary or special-event venues.

Mobile. Whether you're selling to the public or other businesses, if you have a product or service that you take to your customers, your ideal "location" may be a car, van or truck.

Commercial. Commercial space includes even more options than retail. Commercial office buildings and business parks offer traditional office space geared to businesses that do not require a significant amount of pedestrian or automobile traffic for sales. You'll find commercial office space in business districts, parks, and sometimes interspersed among suburban retail facilities.

Industrial. If your business involves manufacturing or heavy distribution, you will need a plant or a warehouse facility. Light industrial parks typically attract smaller manufacturers in non-polluting industries as well as companies that need showrooms in addition to manufacturing facilities.

IT STILL COMES DOWN TO YOU

Technology and statistics are important elements of your site selection decision, but nothing beats your personal involvement in the process. Real estate brokers and economic development agencies can give you plenty of numbers, but remember that their job is to get you to choose their location. To get a balanced picture, take the time to visit the sites yourself, talk to people who own or work in nearby businesses, and verify the facts and what they mean to the potential success of your business.

BUILD A POSITIVE COMPANY IMAGE

It is just not enough to create a terrific product, offer super service and have a solid business plan to back you up. Your company image is equally important to the overall success of your business. Think about it. Every time you hand out your business card, send a letter or welcome a client into your office or store, you are selling someone on your company.

Your business card, letterhead and signage just like traditional print, radio and TV ads—are valuable selling tools. The look of your office also helps "sell" your business by conveying an image, whether it is that of a funky, creative ad agency or a staid, respectable accounting firm.

Fortunately, just because you are a startup company does not mean you have to look like one. Your logo, business card, signage and style are all part of a cohesive image program known as corporate identity. And with the right corporate identity, your company can appear highly professional and give the impression of having been in business for years.

SALES INVENTORY CONTROL

Inventory control doesn't just mean counting. Take physical control of your inventory, too. Lock it up or restrict access. Remember that inventory is money.

There is more to inventory control than simply buying new products. You have to know what to buy when to buy it and how much to buy. You also need to track your inventory whether manually or by computer and use that knowledge to hone your purchasing process.

MAINTAINING ENOUGH INVENTORY

Your business's basic stock should provide a reasonable assortment of products and should be big enough to cover the normal sales demands of your business. Since you won't have actual sales and stocking figures from previous years to guide you during startup, you must project your first year's sales based on your business plan.

When calculating basic stock, you must also factor in lead time, the length of time between reordering and receiving a product. For instance, if your lead time is four weeks and a particular product line sells 10 units a week, then you must reorder before the basic inventory level falls below 40 units. If you do not reorder until you need the stock, you'll have to wait four weeks without the product.

Insufficient inventory means lost sales and costly, time-consuming backorders. Running out of raw materials or parts that are crucial to your production process means increased operating costs, too. One way to protect yourself from shortfalls is by building a safety margin into basic inventory figures. To figure out the right safety margin for your business, try to think of all the outside factors that could contribute to delays, such as suppliers who tend to be late or goods being shipped from overseas. Once you have been in business a while, you'll have a better feel for delivery times and will find it fairly easy to calculate your safety margin.

"The secret of success is to do the common things uncommonly well."
-- John Rockefeller.

Avoiding excess inventory is especially important for owners of companies with seasonal product lines, such as clothing, home accessories, and holiday and gift items. These products have a short "shelf life" and are hard to sell once they are no longer in fashion. Entrepreneurs who sell more timeless products, such as plumbing equipment, office supplies or auto products, have more leeway because it takes longer for these items to become obsolete. To avoid accumulating excess inventory, set a realistic safety margin and order only what you're sure you can sell.

What we think determines what happens to us, so if we want to change our lives, we need to stretch our minds." - Wayne Dyer

TRACKING INVENTORY

A good inventory tracking system will tell you what merchandise is in stock, what is on order when it will arrive and what you've sold. With such a system, you can plan purchases intelligently and quickly recognize the fast-moving items you need to reorder and the slow-moving items you should mark down or specially promote.

You can create your own inventory tracking system or ask your accountant to set one up for you. Systems vary according to the amount of inventory displayed, the amount of backup stock required, the diversity of merchandise, and the number of items that are routinely reordered compared to new items or one-time purchases.

As your business expands and becomes more complex, you'll need more complex inventory techniques to keep up. Tap outside sources to beef up your own and your employees' inventory management expertise. Inexpensive seminars held by banks, consultants and management associations offer a quick but thorough introduction to inventory management techniques.

BUSINESS INSURANCE

One of the most common mistakes startup business owners make is failing to buy adequate insurance for their businesses. It's an easy error to make: Money is tight, and with so many things on your mind, protecting yourself against the possibility of some faraway disaster just doesn't seem that important. "Oh, I will get insurance," you promise yourself, "one of these days."

Soon, "one of these days" comes and goes, and you're still uninsured. Only now, your business has gotten much bigger . . . you've put a lot more into it . . . and you have a lot more to lose. Everything, to be exact.

It doesn't take much. A fire, a burglary, the illness of a key employee—any one of these could destroy everything you've worked so hard to build. When you think of all the time, effort and money you're investing in your business, doesn't it make sense to invest a little extra to protect it?

SPEAK TO YOUR LAWYER AND GET INSURED

SECTION FIVE

USING TECHNOLOGY TO BOOST YOUR PRODUCTIVITY

If you're like most business people, you probably have the main base of operations you call your "office." It may not be an office per say; it could be a retail store, a factory floor, or a trailer on a construction site. It could also be a room in your home or a cubicle within a larger office complex. But it's where you can usually be found from during working hours.

Correction: It used to be where you were usually found. These days, your exact location could vary widely. Nowadays, entrepreneurs and employees alike are just as likely to be found working from home, at a client's office, from a hotel room, or while onboard an aeroplane or train. Widespread use of devices such as iPhones, smartphones, and the latest wireless laptop computers and netbooks means your office can be virtually anywhere, and you can stay connected to your co-workers, clients and customers anywhere, anytime.

Another way to think about it is that, in reality, the office is you or, at the very least, it becomes whatever workspace you happen to be occupying at the moment. Work is now something you do, rather than a place you go to. In today's business world, you're no longer chained to a desk by a fixed phone number (that only rings at your office), and you're not required to use an oversized desktop computer that contains all your important data. Internet connectivity, powerful mobile versions of office tools and new phone services (not to mention the latest cell phones and wireless PDAs) are loosening the ties that bind and making the physical location more about convenience than necessity.

Many entrepreneurs have the equivalent of fully equipped virtual offices in the laptops, and smartphones, they carry around. Some enterprises have even become virtual companies with workmates spending most of their time in separate locations and meeting only occasionally. You're "in the office" whenever you're telecommuting.

The goal isn't to do away with the traditional "office," it's to use networking and communications technologies to turn it into your "extended office." Your extended office isn't a real, physical location; it's virtual, just like the internet is virtual.

You can't touch the internet, even though you can touch one of the servers, routers or fiber optic cables on which it depends. The internet is a convention on which we all agree just as we agree that you're in your extended office when we reach you by cell phone on a Bahamian beach.

People have been teleworking for decades, but our current degree of mobility is a direct outgrowth of the internet and the mobile devices that allow us to easily connect to the internet from anywhere.

CHAPTER EIGHTEEN

BUILD YOUR COMPANY WEBSITE

W hy put your business online? The answer is simple. Because in today's business world, your business must have an online presence if you want to stay competitive. Your prospective and existing customers use the internet for a wide range of purposes, such as researching products they need, then purchasing those items from the comfort of their homes or offices, or anywhere else they may be. Chances are, your competition is already online and is using their internet presence as an extremely powerful sales, marketing, and promotional tool. Being online gives prospective to the customers, offers interactive customer service, allows them to make immediate purchases, and also backs up those sales with technical support.

A web presence allows you to communicate with anyone, anywhere (or thousands of people at once) with e-mail, a blog, an electronic newsletter, or directly through your website. Your website can also be an electronic brochure (that's available 24/7) to show and promote your wares to your target audience

HAVE AN E-COMMERCE PLAN

If you plan to sell anything online, having an e-commerce plan is as important as your original business plan. Because you're exploring new territory, making decisions about technology and marketing, and establishing a new set of vendor relationships, a well-thought-out plan will serve you well.

The first step in writing an e-business plan is to decide what kind of experience you want your online customers to have. Think not only about today but also two and five years down the road.

Your e-commerce plan starts with your website goals. Who are your target customers? What do they need? Are they getting information only, or can they buy products at your site? These key questions asked and answered early, will determine how much time and money you'll need to develop and maintain an online presence.

Second, decide what products or services you will offer. How will you position and display them? Will you offer both online and offline purchasing? How will you handle shipping and returns? Additionally, don't overlook the customer's need to reach a live person. A toll-free phone number should be prominently displayed that customers can call anytime to get their questions answered by a live person.

As you explore the web for vendors to support your e-business, have a clear idea of how you want to handle the "back end" of the business. If you decide to sell online, you'll need a shopping cart component, which is a means of handling credit card processing, and an organized order fulfillment process. However, you may decide that your site is informational only and that you will continue to process transactions offline.

Finally, even if you build an amazing website, don't assume people will find your business on their own. If you simply build it, they will not come. If you want to develop a consistent flow of traffic to your site, it's essential that you plan, execute and maintain an ongoing and multifaceted promotional strategy that's carefully targeted to your audience. This is in addition to the promotions, advertising and marketing you already do for your brick-and-mortar business.

The website should be viewed as an integral part of the marketing effort as another 'front door,' if you will, into the business," says Frank Catalano.

After all, the site is a way to distribute information, gather customer feedback and even sell a product or service. Just promoting a website without regard to overall business goals and other marketing efforts is pointless.

CHAPTER NINETEEN

CHOOSING WEBSITE NAME

Once you've decided to have a website, one of your first "to-do" items is to make a list of possible website names or URLs. Then run, don't walk, to the nearest computer, log on to the internet, go to your favorite search engine, and type in "domain registration."

You will find a list of companies, such as networksolutions.com, godaddy.com and register.com that will guide you through the simple domain registration process. For a modest fee ($8 to $75), you can register a domain name for one or more years. You'll probably discover that GoDaddy.com offers the most competitive rates for domain name registration, plus the widest range of online tools and services that will help you plan, design, publish, manage and promote your online presence.

If the name you decide on is taken, you'll want to have at least two or three backup options. Let's say that you sell flowers, and you would like to register your online name as flowers.com. A search shows that flowers.com is taken. Your second choice is buyflowers.com, but that's already spoken for as well. Many of the domain name registrars, like GoDaddy.com or Register.com, offer several alternatives that are still available, such as buy flowers.tv, buyflowers.cc and buy flowers.ws.

How are these different? Instead of the generic top-level domains (such as .com, .org, .net, or .gov), they include lesser-known and used top-level domain extensions.

The problem with this is that most web surfers automatically type ".com" after the domain name they're looking for. If your competition has flowers.com, but you have flowers.info, you may lose a significant amount of traffic as a result of web surfer confusion. Thus, it's preferable to register a domain name that ends with ".com."

From the available names, choose one that's easy to spell and remember, and describes what your company does. Make sure, however, you're not imposing on someone else's trademark or copyrighted name. In many cases, the name of your company, with the addition of dot-com (www.[YourCompanyName].com) is a suitable domain name that you should definitely register.

If you choose a domain name that's difficult to spell or that might easily be confused with something else, also register the most common misspellings, or what you think people might accidentally type into their browser to find your website. If you don't do this, your competition might, and they could wind up stealing some of your website traffic.

Once you've chosen a name, prompts on the domain registration site will guide you through a simple registration procedure. You'll generally be offered one-, two- or three-year registration packages. Once you pick a domain name and start promoting it, you'll want to stick with it. Otherwise, you'll confuse your customers and could lose web traffic. However, it is appropriate to have several domain names linking to the same website. These different domain names can be used as part of separate marketing and promotional plans that target an audience.

Why is domain name registration imperative? Everyone wants a catchy name, so registering yours ensures that no one else can use it as long as you maintain your registration. For a small investment, you can hold your place on the internet until you're ready to launch.

With your e-commerce name established, start telling people your domain name and promoting it heavily. Make sure you've done everything you can do offline to tell people about your site at the same time you go online. Print your web address on your business cards, brochures, letterhead, invoices and press releases as well as on your product packaging and within product user manuals and advertisements.

Stick it on other items, too, such as mousepads, T-shirts, promotional key chains, and even your company's van.

CHAPTER TWENTY

THE BASICS

O nce you've registered your domain name and have a plan in place for what you want to offer new and existing customers online, the next major challenge is designing and building your actual website or online presence.

A website is typically a collection of individual web pages that are connected with hyperlinks. What makes a good website? Before getting enmeshed in design details, get the big picture by writing a site outline. In addition to basic text, your website can incorporate photos, illustrations, animation, videos, audio clips, music, and a plethora of other multimedia elements or content that will convey your information to your target audience in an easy-to-understand, visually appealing and appropriate manner. The content you develop and publish should directly relate to and help you achieve the goals and objectives you've set for your website.

A well-thought-out site outline includes:

Content. The key to a successful site is content. Give site visitors lots of interesting information, incentives to visit and buy, and ways to contact you. Once your site is up and running, continually update and add fresh content to keep people coming back.

Structure. Decide how many pages to have and how they'll be linked to each other. Choose graphics and icons that enhance the content.

Design. With the content and structure in place, site design comes next. Whether you're using an outside designer or doing it yourself, concentrate on simplicity, readability and consistency. Remember to focus on what you want to accomplish.

Navigation. Make it easy and enjoyable for visitors to browse the site. For example, use no more than two or three links to major areas and never leave visitors at a dead end.

Credibility. This is an issue that shouldn't be lost in the bells and whistles of establishing a website. Your site should reach out to every visitor, telling that person why he/she should buy your product or your service. It should look very professional, and give potential customers the same feeling of confidence they would get with a phone call or face-to-face visit with you. Remind visitors that you don't exist only in cyberspace. Your company's full contact information; company name, complete address, telephone, fax, and e-mail should appear on all or most of your web pages and be displayed prominently on your site's home page.

An outline helps you get the most out of your website design/ e-commerce budget. It will also help you determine whether you, or someone in your company, can design portions of the website, or if you need to solicit outside help. That way, when you hire someone, it will be for only the parts of the job that you'll need to have outsourced.

At this point, you have two options: You can bring your detailed outline to a prospective web designer, or you could go the do-it-yourself route. Once a designer has your outline, the process will be more efficient, but creating a website from scratch can still be costly and time-consuming. Consider researching one of the many websites or e-commerce turnkey solution services, which allow you to design, publish and manage a website or e-commerce site by customizing website templates using online design and management tools. These services are inexpensive, powerful, and allow you to create highly professional websites with no programming skills.

There are only a few possible reasons why you'd want to hire a website designer and/or programmer to have your site created from scratch vs. using a turnkey solution. One reason would be if you absolutely require specialized functionality (either on the front or back end of the site) that isn't offered by the turnkey solutions. Many startups initially spend too much on a custom-designed site that wasn't really required, and, ultimately, regret the decision since their financial resources that could have been put to better use elsewhere. Instead, it's best to rely on an inexpensive turnkey solution for creating, publishing and managing your website.

As your company grows and becomes successful, it's then possible to transition to a custom-designed site, if the need arises. Once you know what tools and resources you'll use to create and manage the site, the next step is to organize your site's potential content into a script. Your script is the numbered pages that outline the site's content and how web pages will flow from one to the next. Page one is your home page, the very first page that site visitors see when they type in your URL. Arrange all the icons depicting major content areas in the order you want them. Pages two through whatever corresponds to each icon on your home page.

Writing a script also ensures your website is chock-full of appropriate content that's well-organized. Offer your visitors content that's valuable, informative and engaging, make it worth their while to spend time on your site. Provide regular opportunities for visitors to get more content. Whether you offer a blog, free electronic newsletter, a calendar of events, columns from experts, or book reviews, your content and the site's structure become the backbone of your website.

As part of your website design, use graphics, colors and fonts that make sense (not just to you but to your target audience as well). Subtle visual cues make all the difference in how visitors respond to your website. Surf the net to research what combinations of fonts, colors and graphics appeal to your audience, and incorporate pleasant and effective design elements into your site.

If your target audience is comprised of a tween or teenage girls, using a color combination of pinks, reds and other feminine or pastel colors, along with more decorative (yet easy-to-read font) makes sense.

However, if you're targeting middle-aged businessmen, a more masculine color scheme, combined with traditional fonts, should be used. To create a successful website, all the elements must work seamlessly. Sure, having top-notch content is essential, but it must be displayed in a manner that's easy to understand, visually appealing, simple to navigate, and of interest to your target audience. How you present your information is important. It's not just about what you have to say, but it's also how you present that content that will either attract or repel your audience.

When creating and designing your web content, you won't go wrong if you follow three basic design rules:

Put the most important pages near the top.

Eliminate extraneous words and visual clutter from the content.

Use headlines, icons, bullets, boldface words and color only to draw attention to important content, not to distract or confuse the web surfer.

DOS AND DON'TS OF SITE DESIGN

For a successful website, follow these general dos and don'ts of site design.

Do:

Make your site easy to navigate.

Use a consistent look, layout, design and feel throughout your site.

Make sure your website works with all the popular web browsers (Explorer, Safari, Foxfire, Chrome, etc.).

Don't:

Use text and color combinations that are too busy or distracting.

Anything that makes your site confusing or hard to read should be eliminated immediately.

Allow the content or links on your website to become outdated; update, fine-tune and proofread regularly.

CHAPTER TWENTY-ONE

PUBLISHING YOUR WEBSITE

N ow that you have your site's design and content creation well underway, the next step is publishing your site on the net. For this, you have three basic options.

The first is to host it yourself on a computer that can be dedicated as a web server (or a computer that's permanently connected to the internet) and has a broadband internet connection. This will prove costly to set up and maintain. For most online businesses, this isn't the best option, at least in the beginning.

The second option is to use an established and reputable web hosting company, which stores and manages websites for businesses, among other services. There are several large and well-established web hosting companies that cater to a worldwide audience, including Yahoo! Google and GoDaddy.com. Some companies, however, prefer local, small-hosting providers, since they offer direct contact especially important if your site goes down.

A third option and the most popular (as well as the least expensive) is to use a website turnkey solution. This is a company that provides all the site development tools and hosting services in one easy-to-use, low cost, bundled service, which is entirely online-based. In other words, to create, publish and manage your website, you don't need to install any specialized software, and no programming is required. Using an internet search engine, enter the phrase "website turnkey solution" or "e-commerce turnkey solution." Also, check out what's offered by Yahoo!, Google, GoDaddy.com and eBay.com. Whether buying from a large or small provider, basic hosting service along with standards like domain name registration and e-mail accounts starts at about $10 per month but can go up considerably, depending on your needs.

Still not sure which host to choose? Log on to Compare Web Hosts (comparewebhosts.com), where you can compare hosts based on price. Other variables include the amount of disk space allocated to you, available bandwidth, number of e-mail services offered, customer service support availability, database support and setup fees.

THE E-COMMERCE NEEDS

The best part of e-commerce is that customers do the work while you make the sales. Many e-commerce entrepreneurs turn to the web hosting companies to solve all their e-commerce needs, such as handling credit card transactions, sending automatic e-mail messages to customers thanking them for their orders, and forwarding the order to them for shipping and handling—and of course, domain registration and hosting.

Another option is to incorporate an electronic shopping cart module, which allows people to place their orders online and process their credit card payment transactions. A site using a shopping cart module should have these four components:

Catalog. Customers can view products, get information and compare prices.

Shopping cart. The icon works like the real thing. It tracks all the items in the basket and can add or delete items as the customer goes along. It's like an online order form.

Checkout counter. The shopper reviews the items in her cart makes changes and decides on shipping preferences, gift-wrapping and the like.

Order processing. The program processes the credit card (or payment option), verifies all information, and sends everything to the database.

THE FINAL CHECK

You're now just about ready to launch your online business (or the online component to your traditional business). Here's a checklist to keep you on track:

Keep your online and e-commerce strategy in focus. Put full contact information on your homepage.

Make sure your online message is clear.

Keep graphics clean and eye-catching.

Make sure your website is free of glitches, typos, and dead ends that frustrate visitors.

Ensure your site meets its objectives.

Enable visitors to get information quickly and easily.

Make sure your website meshes with the rest of your business.

Once your website is up and running, it's time to get to the really important jobs. The first is getting visitors to your site (generating traffic), followed by encouraging them to become paying customers. Promoting and advertising your site properly, and on an ongoing basis, will be essential for its success.

CHAPTER TWENTY-TWO

BUILDING A BRAND

As a startup entrepreneur, you'll be branding whether or not you're even trying. If you don't have a clear idea of what your new company is about, your potential customers will decide on their own, and that's a risky move for a new company without many, or any, customers. You'll need to have a branding strategy in place before you hang up your shingle.

Branding is a very misunderstood term. Many people think of branding as just advertising or a cool-looking logo, but it's much more complex and much more exciting, too.

Branding is your company's foundation. Branding is more than an element of marketing, and it's not just about awareness, a trademark or a logo. Branding is your company's reason for being, the synchronization of everything about your company that leads to consistency for you as the owner, your employees and your potential customers. Branding meshes your marketing, public relations, business plan, packaging, pricing, customers, and employees.

Branding creates value. If done right, branding makes the buyer trust and believe your product is somehow better than those of your competitors. Generally, the more distinctive you can make your brand, the less likely the customer will be willing to use another company's product or service, even if yours is slightly more expensive.

Branding clarifies your message. You have less money to spend on advertising and marketing as a startup entrepreneur, and good branding can help you direct your money more effectively.

Branding is a promise. At the end of the day, branding is the simple, steady promise you make to every customer who walks through your door—today, tomorrow and ten years from now. Your company's ads and brochures might say you offer speedy, friendly service, but if customers find your service slow and surly, they'll walk out the door feeling betrayed.

BRANDING STRATEGY

Your business plan should include a branding strategy. This is your written plan for how you'll apply your brand strategically throughout the company over time. At its core, a good branding strategy lists the one or two most important elements of your product or service, describes your company's ultimate purpose in the world and defines your target customer. The result is a blueprint for what's most important to your company and your customer.

Don't worry; creating a branding strategy isn't nearly as scary or as complicated as it sounds. Here's how:

Step one: Set yourself apart. Why should people buy from you instead of the other business that is the same across town? Think about the intangible qualities of your product or service, using adjectives from "friendly" to "fast" and every word in between. Your goal is to own a position in the customer's mind so they think of you differently than the competition. How will you be different from the competition? The answers are valuable assets that constitute the basis of your brand.

Step two: Know your target customer. Once you've defined your product or service, think about your target customer. You've probably already gathered demographic information about the market you're entering, but think about the actual customers who will walk through your door. Who is this person, and what is the one thing he or she ultimately wants from your product or service? After all, the customer is buying it for a reason. What will your customer demand from you?

Step three: Develop a personality. How will you show customers every day what you're all about? A lot of small companies write mission statements that say the company will "value" customers and strive for "excellent customer service." Unfortunately, these words are all talk and no action. Dig deeper and think about how you'll fulfill your brand's promise and provide value and service to the people you serve. If you promise quick service, for example, what

108

will "quick" mean inside your company? And how will you make sure service stays speedy?

Along the way, you're laying the foundation of your hiring strategy and how future employees will be expected to interact with customers. You're also creating the template for your advertising and marketing strategy. Your branding strategy doesn't need to be more than one page long at most. It can even be as short as one paragraph. It all depends on your product or service and your industry. The important thing is that you answer these questions before you open your doors.

HOW TO MANAGE YOUR BRAND

Keep ads brand-focused. Keep your promotional blitzes narrowly focused on your chief promise to potential customers. For example, a new bakery might see the warmth of its fresh bread as its greatest brand-building asset. Keep your message simple and consistent so people get the same message every time they see your name and logo.

Be consistent. Filter every business proposition through a branding filter. How does this opportunity help build the company's brand? How does this opportunity fit our branding strategy? These questions will keep you focused and put you in front of people who fit your product or service.

Shed the dead weight. Good businesses are willing to change their brands but are careful not to lose sight of their original customer base and branding message. Consider Starbucks, which changed the way it made lattes to speed up the process. "You have to give up something to build a brand," Ries says. "Good brands constantly get rid of things that don't work."

If you can dream it, you can do it." – Walter Elias Disney

SECTION SIX
ADVERTISING AND MARKETING YOUR BUSINESS

Advertising doesn't have to mean multi-million dollar TV commercials. There are plenty of ways to market your business that are affordable or even free. All it takes is a little marketing savvy and the dedication to stick with a year-round program that includes a solid mix of proven tactics. Your business plan and your marketing plan have a lot in common, but make sure to keep them separate. Your business plan should show how you're going to support your marketing efforts. At the same time, your marketing plan should be a concrete working out of the ideas in your business plan.

CHAPTER TWENTY-THREE

CREATE A MARKETING PLAN

U nlike a business plan, a marketing plan focuses on winning and keeping customers. A marketing plan is strategic and includes numbers, facts, and objectives. Marketing supports sales, and a good marketing plan spells out all the tools and tactics you'll use to achieve your sales goals. It's your plan of action that shows what you'll sell, who will want to buy it, and the tactics you'll use to generate leads that result in sales.

And unless you're using your marketing plan to help you gain funding, it doesn't have to be lengthy or beautifully written. Use bulleted sections, and get right to the point.

Step One: Begin with a Snapshot of Your Company's Current Situation, Called a "Situation Analysis" This step defines your company and its products or services, then shows how the benefits you provide set you apart from your competition.

Target audiences have become extremely specialized and segmented. For example, there are hundreds of special-interest magazines each targeted to a specific market segment. No matter your industry, from restaurants to professional services to retail clothing stores, positioning your product or service competitively requires an understanding of your niche market. Not only do you need to be able to describe what you market, but you must also have a clear understanding of what your competitors are offering and be able to show how your product or service provides a better value.

Make your Situation Analysis a succinct overview of your company's strengths, weaknesses, opportunities and threats. Strengths and weaknesses refer to characteristics that exist within your business, while opportunities and threats refer to outside factors. Positioning your product involves two steps. First, you need to analyze your product's features and decide how they

111

distinguish your product from its competitors. Second, decide what type of buyer is most likely to purchase your product. What are you selling convenience? Quality? Discount pricing? You can't offer it all. Knowing what your customers wants helps you decide what to offer, and that also brings us to the next section of your plan.

Step Two: Describe Your Target Audience. Developing a simple, one-paragraph profile of your prospective customer is the second step in an effective marketing plan. You can describe prospects in terms of demographics, age, sex, family composition, earnings and geographic location as well as lifestyle. Ask yourself the following: Are my customers conservative or innovative? Leaders or followers? Timid or aggressive? Traditional or modern? Introverted or extroverted? How often do they purchase what I offer? In what quantity? The more narrowly you define your target audience, the less money you'll waste on ads and PR in poorly targeted media and the unqualified leads they would generate.

Step Three: List Your Marketing Goals. What do you want your marketing plan to achieve? For example, are you hoping for a 20 per cent increase in sales of your product per quarter? Write down a shortlist of goals and make them measurable so that you'll know when you've achieved them.

Step Four: Develop the Marketing Communications Strategies and the Tactics. You'll Use. This section is the heart and soul of your marketing plan. Now it's time to detail the tactics you'll use to reach these prospects and accomplish your goals. A good marketing program targets prospects at all stages of your sales cycle. Some marketing tactics such as many forms of advertising, public relations, and direct marketing are great for reaching cold prospects. To complete your tactics section, outline your primary marketing strategies, then include a variety of tactics you'll use to reach prospects at any point in your sales cycle. For example, you might combine outdoor billboards, print advertising and online local searches to reach cold prospects but use e-mail to contact your warm prospects. Finally, you can use one-on-one meetings to close the sale. Don't overlook complementary materials that support sales: For instance, if you plan to meet with prospects to follow up on leads you've generated, you'll need brochures and presentation materials.

To identify your ideal marketing mix, find out which media your target audience turns to for information on the type of product or service you sell. Avoid broad-based media even if it attracts your target audience if the content is not relevant. The marketing tactics you choose must reach your prospects when they'll be most receptive to your message.

Step Five: Set Your Marketing Budget. You'll need to devote a percentage of projected gross sales to your annual marketing budget. Of course, when starting a business this may mean using newly acquired funding, borrowing or self-financing. Just bear this in mind marketing is essential to the success of your business. And with so many different kinds of tactics available for reaching out to every conceivable audience niche, there's a mix to fit even the tightest budget.

Lastly; Dream the dream. Your marketing plan should include a "blue sky" section in which you put your feet back and look at where you think you'll be in a couple of years. Especially in small businesses, it's a waste of time to formulate marketing thoughts that go out more than two or three years. But dreams are important and they can be fun, too.

CHAPTER TWENTY-FOUR

ADVERTISING METHODS

The **print ad** is the basic unit of advertising, the fountainhead from which all other forms of advertising spring

Many entrepreneurs believe that **TV and radio advertising** are beyond their means. But while advertising nationally on commercial network TV may be too costly for many entrepreneurs, advertising on local stations and especially on cable TV can be surprisingly affordable. Armed with the right information, you may find that TV and radio advertising deliver more customers than any other type of ad campaign. The key is to have a clear understanding of your target audience and what they want or listen to so the money spent on broadcast advertising is invested in programming that reaches them in the right way and the right context.

Direct mail encompasses a wide variety of marketing materials, including brochures, catalogs, postcards, newsletters and sales letters. Major corporations know that direct-mail advertising is one of the most effective and profitable ways to reach out to new and existing clients. What's the advantage? Unlike other forms of advertising, in which you're never sure just who is getting your message, direct mail lets you communicate one-on-one with your target audience. That allows you to control who receives your message, when it is delivered, what is in the envelope, and how many people you reach.

Classified ads are a smart way to reach prospects who are looking for and are prepared to buy what you sell. And since they demand neither the eye-catching design of a display ad nor the clever wording of a direct-mail campaign, almost anyone can write them.

Co-op advertising is a cooperative advertising effort between suppliers and retailers such as between a soda company and a convenience store that advertises the company's products.

MEASURE THE EFFECTIVENESS OF YOUR ADS

Check the effectiveness of your advertising programs regularly by conducting one or more of the following tests:

Run the same ad in two different publications with a different identifying mark on each one. Ask customers to clip the ad and bring it in for a discount or a free sample.

Train everyone in your company who answers the phone to ask customers where they heard about you.

Offer a product at different prices in different magazines. This has the added benefit of showing whether consumers will buy your product at a higher price.

Advertise an item in one ad only. Don't have any signs or otherwise promote the item in your store or business.

Stop running an ad that you regularly run. See if dropping the ad affects sales.

Always check sales results. This is especially important when you place an ad for the first time.

Check-in like these will give you some idea of how your advertising and marketing program is working. Be aware, however, that you can't expect immediate results from an ad. Advertising consistently is important, especially if you run small-space ads, which are less likely to be seen and remembered than larger ads.

EFFECTIVE SELLING TECHNIQUES

No matter what business you're in, if you're an entrepreneur, you're in sales. "But I hate to sell," you groan. You're not alone. Many people are intimidated by selling either because they're not sure how to proceed or they think they don't have the "right" personality to sell. Well, guess what? Anyone can sell anything to anyone, this is an individual who can learn to connect with the customer, listen to his or her needs and offer the right solutions.

Understanding Your Unique Selling Proposition

Before you can begin to sell your product or service to anyone else, you have to sell yourself on it. This is especially important when your product or service is similar to those around you. Very few businesses are one of a kind. Just look around you: How many clothing retailers, hardware stores, air conditioning installers and electricians are truly unique?

The key to effective selling in this situation is what advertising and marketing professionals call a "unique selling proposition" (USP). Unless you can pinpoint what makes your business unique in a world of homogeneous competitors, you cannot target your sales efforts successfully.

Pinpointing your USP requires some hard soul-searching and creativity. One way to start is to analyze how other companies use their USPs to their advantage. This requires careful analysis of other companies' ads and marketing messages. If you analyze what they say they sell, not just their product or service characteristics, you can learn a great deal about how companies distinguish themselves from competitors.

For example, Charles Revson, founder of Revlon, always used to say he sold hope, not the makeup. Some airlines sell friendly service, while others sell on-time service. Neiman Marcus sells luxury, while Walmart sells bargains. Each of these is an example of a company that has found a USP "peg" on which to hang its marketing strategy. A business can peg its USP on product characteristics, price structure, placement strategy (location and distribution) or promotional strategy known as the 4Ps.

Here's how to uncover your USP and use it to power up your sales:

Put yourself in your customer's shoes. Too often, entrepreneurs fall in love with their product or service and forget that it is the customer's needs, not their own, that they must satisfy. Step back from your daily operations and carefully scrutinize what your customers want. Suppose you own a pizza parlor. Sure, customers come into your pizza place for food. But is food all they want? What could make them come back again and again and ignore your competition? The

116

answer might be quality, convenience, reliability, friendliness, cleanliness, courtesy or customer service.

Remember, price is never the only reason people buy. If your competition is beating you on pricing because they are larger, you have to find another sales feature that addresses the customer's needs and then build your sales and promotional efforts around that feature.

Know what motivates your customers' behavior and buying decisions. Effective marketing requires you to be an amateur psychologist. You need to know what drives and motivates customers. Go beyond the traditional customer demographics such as age, gender, race, income, and geographic location that most businesses collect to analyze their sales trends. For our pizza parlor example, it is not enough to know that 75 per cent of your customers are in the 18-to-25 age range. You need to look at their motives for buying pizza; taste, peer pressure, convenience and so on. Cosmetics and liquor companies are great examples of industries that know the value of the psychologically oriented promotion. People buy these products based on their desires (for pretty women, luxury, glamour and so on), not on their needs.

Uncover the real reasons customers buy your product instead of a competitor's. As your business grows, you'll be able to ask your best source of information: your customers. For example, the pizza entrepreneur could ask them why they like his/her pizza over others, plus ask them to rate the importance of the features he offers, such as taste, size, ingredients, atmosphere and service. You will be surprised at how honest people are when you ask how you can improve your service. Since your business is just starting out, you won't have a lot of customers to ask yet, so "shop" your competition instead. Many retailers routinely drop into their competitors' stores to see what and how they are selling. If you are really brave, try asking a few of the customers after they leave the premises what they like and dislike about the competitors' products and services.

Once you have gone through this three-step market intelligence process, you need to take the next and hardest step: *clearing your mind of any preconceived ideas about your product or service and being brutally honest.* What features of your business jump out at you as something that sets you apart? What can you promote that will make customers want to patronize your business? How can you position your business to highlight your USP?

Do not get discouraged. Successful business ownership is not about having a unique product or service; it's about making your product stand out, even in a market filled with similar items.

CHAPTER TWENTY-FIVE

MAKING SALES PRESENTATIONS

You have made an appointment to visit a prospect in person and make a sales presentation. How can you make sure it's a success? Four elements determine whether a sale will be made or not:

1. **Rapport:** putting yourself on the same side of the fence as the prospect

2. **Need:** determining what factors will motivate the prospect to listen with the intent to purchase

3. **Importance**: the weight the prospect assigns to a product, feature, benefit, price or time frame

4. **Confidence**: your ability to project credibility, to remove doubt, and to gain the prospect's belief that the risk of purchase will be less than the reward of ownership.

Here is a closer look at the steps you can take to make your sales presentation a success.

Step 1: Before the Presentation

Know your customer's business. Potential clients expect you to know their business, customers, and competition as well as you know your own product or service. Study your customer's industry. Know its problems and trends. Find out who the company's biggest competitors are.

Write out your sales presentation. Making a sales presentation isn't something you do on the fly. Always use a written presentation. The basic structure of any sales presentation includes five key points: Build rapport with your prospect, introduce the business topic, ask questions to better understand your prospect's needs, summarize your key selling points, and close the sale. Think about the three major selling points of your product or service. Develop leading questions to probe your customer's reactions and needs.

Make sure you are talking to the right person. When you are setting the appointment, always ask "Are you the one I should be talking to, or are there others who will be making the buying decision?"

Step 2: In the Customer's Office

Build rapport. Before you start discussing business, build rapport with your prospect. To accomplish this, do some homework. Find out if you have a colleague in common. Has the prospect's company been in the news lately? Is he or she interested in sports? Get a little insight into the company and the individual so you can make the rapport genuine.

Ask questions. The most effective way to sell is to ask the prospect questions and see where he or she leads you. Ask questions that require more than a yes or no response and that deal with more than just costs, price, procedures, and the technical aspects of the prospect's business. Most importantly ask questions that will reveal the prospect's motivation to purchase, his or her problems and needs, and the prospect's decision-making processes. Don't be afraid to ask a client why he or she feels a certain way. That's how you'll get to understand your customers.

Take notes. Don't rely on your memory to remind you of what's important to your prospect. Ask upfront if it's all right for you to take notes during your sales presentation. Prospects will be flattered. Write down key points you can refer to later during your presentation. Be sure to write down objections.

Learn to listen. Sales people who do all the talking during a presentation not only bore the prospect but also generally lose the sale. A good rule of thumb is to listen to 70 per cent of the time and talk 30 per cent of the time. Don't interrupt. It's tempting to step in and tell the prospect something you think is vitally important. Before you speak, ask yourself if what you're about to say is necessary.

Answer objections with "feel," "felt" and "found." Don't argue when a prospect says "I'm not interested," "I just bought one," or "I don't have time right now." Simply say "I understand how you feel.

Probe deeper. Asking for more information and listening to the answers enables you to better position your product and show you understand the client's needs.

Find the "hot button." A customer may have a long list of needs, but there is usually one "hot button" that will get the person to buy. The key to the hot button is that it is an emotional, not practical, but a need for recognition, love or reinforcement.

Eliminate objections. When a prospect objects, don't immediately jump in with a response. Instead, show empathy by saying "Let's explore your concerns." Ask for more details about the objection. You need to isolate the true objection so you can handle it.

119

Close the sale. There is no magic to closing the sale. If you have followed all the previous steps, all you should have to do is ask for the customer's order. However, some salespeople make the mistake of simply not asking for the final decision. It's as if they forget what their goal is! For some, "closing" sounds too negative. If you're one of them, try changing your thinking to something more positive, such as "deciding." As you talk with the customer, build in the close by having fun with it. Say something like "So how many do you want? We have it in a rainbow of colors; do you want them all?" Make sure to ask them several times in a fun, nonthreatening way; you're leading them to make the decision.

Step 3: After the sale

Follow up. What you do after the sale is just as crucial as what you did to get it.

Ask for feedback. Ask customers what you need to do to maintain and increase their business.

SPEAKING EFFECTIVELY

The difference between good and great salespeople is the way they deliver their messages. You can have the greatest sales pitch in the world, but if you deliver it with no enthusiasm, sincerity or belief, you will lose the sale.

Here are some suggestions to improve your speaking skills and power up your presentations:

Speak clearly. If the prospect doesn't understand you, you won't get the sale.

Lean forward. Leaning into the presentation gives the prospect a sense of urgency.

Don't fidget. Knuckle-cracking, hair-twirling and similar nervous habits detract from your presentation.

Don't "um," "ah" or "er." These vocal tics are so irritating, they make the prospect focus on the flaws rather than the message. Best cure? Practice, practice, practice. Be animated. Act as if the best thing in the world just happened to you.

Vary your voice. Don't drone on in a monotone. Punch the critical words. Go from high to low tones. Whisper some of the key information as if it's a secret. Get the prospect to lean into your words. Make him or her feel fortunate to be receiving this message.

Look prospects in the eye. Eye contact signals credibility and trustworthiness.

Follow the prospect's lead. Keep your tone similar to his or her tone. If the prospect is stuffy and conservative, do not get too wild.

Relax. High anxiety makes prospects nervous. Why do salespeople get nervous? Either they are unprepared or they need the money from the sale. Calm down. Never let them see you sweat.

Sell benefits, not features. The biggest mistake entrepreneurs make is focusing on what their product or service is (its features). Rather, it's what it does (its benefits) that's important. For example, a health-food product contains nutrients that are good for the body. That's what it is. What the product does is make the customer thinner, more energetic, and able to do more with less sleep.

CHAPTER TWENTY-SIX

OFFERING TOP NOTCH CUSTOMER SERVICE

To the ordinary entrepreneur, closing and finalizing the sale is the completion of serving the customer's needs. But for the pro, this is only the beginning. Closing the sale sets the stage for a relationship that, if properly managed by you, the entrepreneur, can be mutually profitable for years to come.

Remember the "80–20 rule"; The rule states that 80 per cent of your business comes from 20 per cent of your customers. Repeat customers are the backbone of every successful business. So now that you know how to land customers, it is time to learn how to keep them.

Building Customer Relationships

It's tempting to concentrate on making new sales or pursuing bigger accounts. But attention to your existing customers, no matter how small they are, is essential to keeping your business thriving. The secret to repeat business is following up in a way that has a positive effect on the customer.

Effective follow-up begins immediately after the sale when you call the customer to say "thank you" and find out if he or she is pleased with your product or service. And also remember special occasion like send regular customers birthday cards or gifts.

With all that your existing customers can do for you, there's simply no reason not to stay in regular contact with them. Use your imagination, and you'll think of plenty of other ideas that can help you develop a lasting relationship.

Customer Service

There are plenty of things you, the entrepreneur, can do to ensure good customer service. And when you're a one-person business, it's easy to stay on top of what your customers want. But as you add employees, whether it's one person or 100, you are adding more links to the customer service chain and creating more potential for poor service along the way. That's why creating a customer service policy and adhering to it is so important. Here are some steps you can take to ensure that your clients receive excellent service every step of the way.

Put your customer service policy in writing. These principles should come from you, but every employee should know what the rules are and be ready to live up to them.

Establish support systems that give the employees clear instructions for gaining and maintaining service superiority. These systems will help you out-service any competitor by giving more to customers and anticipating problems before they arise.

Develop a measurement of superb customer service. Then reward employees who practice it consistently.

Be certain that your passion for customer service runs rampant throughout your company. Your employees should see how good service relates to your profits and their future with the company.

Be genuinely committed to providing more customer service excellence than anyone else in your industry. This commitment must be so powerful that every one of your customers can sense it.

Share information with people on the front lines. Meet regularly to talk about improving service. Solicit ideas from employees, they are the ones who are dealing with the customers most often.

Act on the knowledge that customers value attention, competence, promptness and dependability. They love being treated as individuals and being referred to by name. (Don't you?)

Make it easy for customers to contact you by phone, fax or e-mail to share ideas, frustrations and suggestions.

MANAGING CUSTOMER

When most entrepreneurs start their business, they take every customer they can get. In other words, we have all had clients who take advantage of us, and we allow them to do so. In some cases, this situation can be perfectly fine, but it is not ideal when your business loses money. Frequently, we only realize at the point of no return that the unfavorable situation in which we find ourselves could have been avoided; we could have passed on the customer altogether.

Deciding to pass on a customer is especially difficult for young or new entrepreneurs who are hungry for business and revenues. However, choosing bad customers can cause a lot of frustration, drain resources, damage your reputation, and eventually put you out of business.

To help you decide what customers are worth your time, consider four important signs which indicate that you should not take a client and gracefully move on from the relationship. These signs apply especially to entrepreneurs who run a service-oriented or consulting business.

Be skeptical of a client who seems not to know what is needed or who constantly makes changes. For example, if you have a web or graphic design company, explain clearly your creative process and the time needed for the project. Quantify all expectations. Some designers, for instance, agree to do three prototypes. Afterwards, the client must choose from those three prototypes. Avoid at all costs a situation in which you are designing or creating indefinitely, only to have the client choose the tenth iteration. Also, a client should be comfortable with your capabilities and what to expect from you. Find out from new clients what attracted them to your work. Show your portfolio.

Be careful if a client is not willing to pay an hourly rate or a piece rate of some kind. Agreeing to a fixed cost for your work is not bad per say. However, it's not so great if you end up doing more work than you anticipated. Many clients encourage you to lower your cost to lock in a good rate. In a gesture of good faith, sometimes the client will pay you all the money upfront. That way, you are beholden to the client until it receives a deliverable it likes. These types of arrangements can be especially stressful and strain a relationship to the point of litigation.

Avoid any client who hesitates to sign a well-written agreement. This is a true test of whether a client is worth your time and effort. An agreement or contract protects both parties and outlines expectations. Without a comprehensive agreement, you have no way to protect your interests, assess the progress of the work you have done, and verify the deliverable.

Take heed of any less than good feelings you have about a potential client. I have learned to accept my business intuition, and I would say that 80 per cent of the time it leads me to make better decisions about a potential client's value. Don't be afraid to fire a client. Just because some customers want you doesn't mean you need them.

CHAPTER TWENTY-SEVEN

ADS AND ONLINE MARKETING

T hink of your website as a marketing tool like the others you use to promote your business. Because its return is hard to gauge, your job is to learn how to get the most from the web. "Why would someone want to visit my site?" That's your key question. If your site talks only about your company and how great you are, chances are, no one will come back. Attracting visitors requires magnets: things that excite people and make them return for more.

Savvy marketers master permission marketing, which provides incentives for customers to learn more about your product or service. Let's say you run the Clicks and Bricks Bed and Breakfast in Vermont. Spring and fall are your off-seasons. You'd like to reach out to former visitors and those who have sent e-mails inquiring about the Clicks and Bricks B&B.

Using the principles of permission marketing, you can:

Use your database of customer and prospect e-mails to build an audience for a promotional campaign.

Recognize that those consumers have indicated a willingness to talk to you. So find something to say to them. You could offer them a "three nights for the price of two" promotion or run a contest for a free two-night midweek stay. It offers like these that keep customers and prospects engaged.

Encourage a learning relationship with your customers. Send e-mails or print brochures about upcoming local events such as the annual Fuzzy Worm Festival, or offer two-for-one coupons for an upcoming art show. Remind them of Vermont's allure in the spring and fall.

Deepen your communication as site visitors become customers and first-timers become return visitors. Send birthday or anniversary cards. Reward them with a glossy national B&B directory. Show them that you value their patronage.

Before you publicize your site, make sure you have an opt-in box on the home page and throughout your site by using e-mail capture software, also called an autoresponder system. This is a great way to develop customers and build your e-mail list so you can send them valuable offers, tips and resources.

ATTRACTING VISITORS TO YOUR SITE

The number of websites is well over the million marks and crossing into the billions. With millions of websites out there, getting visitors to your individual site is often the biggest challenge.

Your strategies for doing so may include search engines, paid search services and affiliates. Let's consider them one at a time.

Search Engines; Relevancy" is based on how well your offer or site matches the keywords. Your site should include the keyword, or be as close as possible to the keyword that's being searched. Finally, your "content" should address the question being asked. Your goal is to answer the query as directly as possible. Search engine marketing (SEM) is also a rapidly growing and profitable segment of the internet and most searches take place on the following sites; Google.com, Yahoo.com, Bing.com, Ask.com and so on.

Paid Search Services. Many companies are also using paid search services as a supplement to SEM. These services allow you to pay to have your website be part of the results of a user's query on a search engine site. There are three types of paid search services: paid submission, pay-for-inclusion and pay-for-placement.

Affiliates. Firms that sell products and services on their websites for commissions offer another way to draw site visitors. Affiliates place merchant promotions on their websites to sell goods or services. They control the type of promotion, location on the site, and the length of time it runs. In return, the affiliate earns a commission on click-throughs, leads or purchases made through the site.

KEEPING VISITORS AT YOUR SITE

Good website design and strategy for attracting visitors can take you three-quarters of the way to success. The final step is getting people to try your offerings and to come back for more. The best way to do that is to treat each customer as unique. Fortunately, the web lends itself to the kind of personalization that's relatively easy and inexpensive for even the smallest business.

With a little effort, you can address each site visitor's needs effectively. Combined with offline strategic work such as hitting customers every other week with a free newsletter or offering them a two-for-one special if they haven't visited your site in two months, readily available e-commerce tools enable you to personalize as nothing else can.

SECTION SEVEN
AN ENTREPRENEUR'S ATTITUDE
ADAPT TO CHANGE

The average lifespan of a Fortune 500 company is getting shorter and shorter, largely because of the ascendancy of disruptive technologies and companies. Small and nimble start-ups are often overlooked by big corporations and now have the ability with little resources to topple billion-dollar companies.

Substantive data show the increased attrition rate of big companies. An analysis of the major stock market indexes over the past few decades reveals that companies have shorter runs. What does this mean? Many things, but a closer look at the index's rejects sheds light on why companies were removed: Many of the companies vanished for failing to adapt to changing times and evolving with customer demands. Thus, it's safe to say that companies that do not embrace change and reinvent themselves are headed out of business fast.

Change is inevitable, but it is not easy. One of my favorite speakers and authors, Don Hutson, said this about change: "Change happens when the pain to stay the same exceeds the pain to change." Although Hutson was speaking to a group of individuals interested in improving themselves, the same principle applies to business. A business that doesn't change or reinvent itself periodically will experience the pain of bankruptcy.

At that grim point, change is the only option.

Companies that have reached a degree of success are most likely to resist change and to stretch their pain threshold. If something is not broken, don't try to fix it, right? Wrong. There are countless examples of large companies that dominated the market for long periods, but now are struggling just to stay alive. A prime example is Sears Roebuck and Co., which dominated the retail market for decades. Now it struggles to turn a profit. Sears rested on its laurels and missed opportunities to conquer the new business frontier in the 1990s: e-commerce. To Sears's great misfortune, competitors like Amazon.com and Walmart aggressively pursued the retail market and are now winning big.

The question then becomes: How do you manage and cope with change, especially as times and technology move so fast? Companies have faced the challenge of staying relevant and keeping up with the times. This can be achieved by using a basic strategy that minimizes the risk of your company becoming complacent and unwilling to change.

Conduct regular researches on your company as if the business is going to be obsolete in one to two years. To anticipate where the market is going and where you should invest, you can do a bimonthly review and a report of all our systems and processes. The review allows you to identify and adapt to potential disruptions like new technology and competition. For example, the division heads of your company provide a review and a report on how we can improve our products and services even if they are selling well.

You also scan the competitive landscape to find any innovations that are threatening. In addition, identify new technologies and resources that help can help your company to stay ahead of the change curve. A recent company review, for instance, revealed how you can use Pinterest, a social media platform that became popular in 2012, to target new segments in marketing campaigns that normally would be overlooked.

Waiting puts you at a huge disadvantage.

This review and report process is one of the simplest ways to proactively seek change and to reinvent the way you do business, preventing you from becoming complacent and more vulnerable to obsolescence.

A business that ignores change is a business that welcomes its own extermination. The products or services you offer today won't keep you in business tomorrow. The very nature of business includes changing to meet customers' demands in a better way. You have to be strategically proactive in dealing with change in your business, save yourself from a sudden shock and slow death it will have on your company.

EMBRACE TECHNOLOGY
The most challenging thing to do in business is to stay in business. According to the U.S. Department of Commerce, "Seven out of 10 new employer firms survive at least 2 years, half at least 5 years, a third at least 10 years, and a quarter stay in business 15 years or more." As time increases, the odds of your company surviving decrease.

Time seems to be the common dooming factor for thousands of businesses, but a much more devastating agent is at work here, especially nowadays. That agent is technology. At a recent technology conference in Atlanta, Carlos Dominguez, senior vice president at Cisco, discussed how things that used to

128

take a long time now happen quickly and effortlessly. One of his examples shows cased the power of social media and its ability to spread information at unprecedented speeds. He related a story of how he used Twitter to avoid an immediate travel disaster in Mexico. He ended the series, declaring, "Times are exponential." I couldn't agree more. Technological innovation, whether rapid progress in computer science or nanotechnology, is seemingly causing the condensation of time. It is also driving many people out of business.

As an entrepreneur, you must be well aware of technology's power to alter your business. On the one hand, ignoring technology can mean the quick demise of your business. On the other hand, if you adopt it early, it can catapult your business to tremendous growth. One way to stay on top of technological innovation is to implement strategies that promote and reward forward-thinking in your company.

In his excellent book Jump the Curve, futurist Jack Uldrich discusses strategies to survive what he calls an "exponential economy," an economy driven by technological innovation. With compelling cases and commonsense analogies, he urges readers to stay ahead of the curve, referring to the curve on an exponential graph. One of his most convincing strategies is to think rationally about the implications of future-generation technology. To illustrate his point, he uses the case of Reed

Hastings, founder of Netflix. Hastings, a former Peace Corps volunteer, realized after seeing DVD technology in 1996 that data storage would make huge advances. (It certainly did.) As a result, Hastings founded Netflix in 1999 and has grown his company to become a billion-dollar behemoth. Netflix continues to be an industry leader in the video/home rental market. Uldrich would say that Hastings was able to "jump the curve."

FOLLOW UP

Success comes from taking the initiative and following up – Anthony Robbins

The classic case of an entrepreneur failing to follow up is a simple mistake that can have devastating consequences. It's a simple fact: Those who master the art of following up are more successful than those who do not, yet so many entrepreneurs overlook and underestimate this simple rule. Why?

Fear of rejection causes many entrepreneurs to fail to follow up. Learning how to deal with rejection years ago could be difficult as a young entrepreneur. Having to sell my ideas to others was frightening and quite frankly it still is sometimes. No one likes being rejected, but you must get over this fear. I often interpret NO as meaning "not right now." When you follow up with people, especially during a sales call or a negotiation, do it with complete confidence. If you receive a NO, ask open-ended questions to learn why the situation didn't turn out the way you wanted. For example, if someone doesn't want to buy your product, ask, "What was the determining factor in your decision?" Turn a negative into a positive.

Entrepreneurs lack the dedication and energy to follow up. Following up takes concerted effort and planning. Committed to a successful outcome, you can put on your calendar to follow up with your contact every week. A customer relationship management tool to assist you in following up regularly with people who can help you simplifies the task.

A misunderstanding of business etiquette prevents many entrepreneurs from following up. The entrepreneur who commits this error is self-absorbed, following up but doing a lousy job at it. An entrepreneur might assume that the contact should always take the next step. Meanwhile, budget planning periods pass, investment priorities change, and contacts leave the company, and so on. On the contrary, the entrepreneur who calls back several times, ignoring the "volley protocol," more often gets the prize. Sometimes people simply forget or want you to do all the work, but that's sometimes a small price to pay for a big payoff.

In summary, don't let these three common reasons for failing to follow up cripple you. Entrepreneurs don't miss opportunities; they seize them. The surest way to do this is to follow up with everybody, especially people who can help your business excel.

You must remain focused on your journey to greatness – Les Brown

COMFORT ZONE

Too often, entrepreneurs operate solely within the confines of their industries. They socialize with the same type of people, go to the same kinds of places, eat the same foods, visit the same websites, read the same books, and speak the same lingo. Or it could be that entrepreneurs are focused on their businesses so much that they don't take time to do something totally unrelated to what they usually do. Immerse yourself in your industry and focus on it, but step away once in a while, too. If you don't, you could be missing out on a monumental, inspirational moment that takes your business to global heights.

Whenever you have the chance to travel, do so. International travel is great, but inspiration can also come from a day trip to another city in your state or country. Seeing how people do things in a different environment sparks creativity.

Stepping outside of your immediate box, whether it's your office or home, also helps to foster inspiration. If you are stumped or experience some sort of a mental block, you take a walk or do an activity that engages another part of your brain or body. While the focus has been on changing your scenery for inspiration, exploring new activities is just as important and effective. Ideas for that new business may come from the most extraneous experiences.

Placing yourself in new environments and exploring new things enables you to apply those experiences to other facets of life. You become a synthesizer, a skill that, honed properly, could be the key to your next big opportunity in business.

RESPOND QUICKLY TO CUSTOMER'S COMPLAINS

Most importantly, formalize the way you handle urgent, customer complaints. Use this simple five-step process:

Respond quickly and calmly.

Listen attentively after you offer a sincere apology.

Tell the customer how you plan to address the problem in detail with a specific time frame.

Give updates often on the progress of your resolution.

When the issue is resolved, make sure the customer is satisfied.

Not only will this process help you to handle similar problems professionally, but it will also provide a guideline by which you can evaluate the effectiveness of your response. To be great in business means to be great at putting out fires quickly. They are inevitable, and one of the biggest fires you'll have to put out is an urgent customer complaint. Making sure that you resolve customer complaints in the best way possible, to ensure that customers stay with your company, should not be something you learn while on the job if you can help it. Prepare for the fire, and your chances of avoiding a customer conflagration will be much better.

FORMAL EDUCATION

When you become an entrepreneur, your education is just beginning. In fact, to be at the top of your game, you must continually seek and devour information that will make you and your business better. An entrepreneur who stops learning stops earning.

Unfortunately, most secondary schools and colleges don't teach how to attain entrepreneurial success. For this reason, some of the most successful entrepreneurs left school early, eager to gain real-world experience. Entrepreneurs educate themselves primarily through reading books, studying successful people, perusing industry magazines, attending conferences, and countless other ways.

NO COLD CALLS

At a recent entrepreneurship conference where there was a panel with angel investors, an audience member asked the following questions, "Do you make cold calls? And if you do, what should I, as a business owner seeking capital, say?" One of the panelists, Valerie Gaydos, founder and president of Capital Growth, answered the question like most people would expect an angel investor to. She responded that she doesn't take cold calls. Instead, she screens potential companies with her partners who bring her quality companies. However, Timothy Reese, managing partner and general manager of Forge Intellectual

Capital, surprised everyone by saying, "I do take cold calls, but your call shouldn't be cold." Everyone in the audience perked up to hear his advice on how to effectively reach out to an angel investor who knows nothing about you or your company.

When giving his candid advice, Reese emphasized that you must first know as much about his company as possible. For instance, if you are looking for an investment in your apparel company and his firm doesn't invest in those types of companies, you are wasting your time. You must research the types of deals that an angel has done and prefers so that you have a better chance of catching the angel's attention. Furthermore, you should know the size of the deals, and if the information is available, how those deals were structured. It requires quite a bit of research and hard work on your end, but as another angel, Daymond John, on the panel mentioned, this could be the big deal of your life. You don't want to go in totally cold and "botch" the opportunity.

If you are an elite entrepreneur, you don't go into anything cold. Whether you are selling a product or selling your company to an investor, you should know as much as you can about the prospect. Nowadays, there is no excuse for being unprepared. A plethora of informational resources are at hand, the Internet being the most common. Entrepreneurs who go the extra mile to better position themselves in a sale always come out better than an entrepreneur who tries to wing it. The biggest benefit of doing your homework is instantly establishing trust and credibility with your prospect, which goes a long way. As angel investor Reese suggested in his advice, an entrepreneur who approaches him and knows his background instantly earns his respect and ear.

Likewise, your cold calls can warm up quickly when you've researched your prospects thoroughly. They will appreciate your efforts to understand their position. Here's one technique that exhibits how you can establish rapport when making cold calls. Don't focus only on yourself or your product when you communicate with a prospect for the first time. Instead, mention the vital information that your research revealed. For illustration purposes, let's say that your investigation uncovered the prospect's previous buying history and their need to cut costs.

You could start a conversation by saying, "I understand that you have purchased from company A in the past, but I would love to share with you how our product has been rated the highest quality by an independent source and it costs less." By saying this, you've done two important things: earned trust by reviewing the prospect's buying history and sparked interest with a way to reduce cost. Using techniques like this gives you a great advantage over your competition.

The likelihood of closing a sale is directly linked to the preparation that goes into making that sale. Before you attempt to persuade any prospect your way, take the time to find out as much as you can about the person. You'll never have a cold call again.

NEVER TOO LATE TO BE AN ENTREPRENEUR
You are never too old to set another goal or to dream a new dream. -- C. S. Lewis,

As the media focus on young CEOs like Facebook's Mark Zuckerberg and Instagram's Kevin Systrom, it is easy to assume that most companies these days are started by teenagers and people in their twenties. Consequently, many older people buy into this media hype and think that starting a company is for young people, accepting that their chances of success are limited by their age. This assumption and the media hype couldn't be further from the truth.

First, the media hype is heavily focused on the technology sector, which tends to glorify young superstars. When it comes to what is most appealing to the media, the new social media company always overshadows the new bakery on Main Street.

Second, older people are starting more businesses than people in their teens and twenties. According to a Kauffman Foundation study, Americans between the ages of thirty-five and forty-four represented the largest increase in entrepreneurial activity from 2008 to 2009. Americans between ages fifty-five and sixty-four constituted the second-largest jump. The reasons range from middle-aged adults wanting to supplement their income to retired individuals wanting to continue working. Regardless of the reasons, older people are catching the entrepreneurial bug, which is good news for everyone. Unfortunately, we don't hear enough about these exciting data.

Interestingly, research shows that older people are more likely to be successful when they start businesses. Older entrepreneurs have the experience needed to better navigate the rough waters of entrepreneurship. During years of work, they have developed a treasure chest of skills that makes them highly valued. For instance, if they go into business in the same industry in which they worked for many years, their understanding of the business is a tremendous competitive advantage.

In other good news, University of Chicago economist David Galenson contends that "experimental innovators" require time to reach their peak. His research, which is largely credited with cracking the code of the creative mind, concludes that experimental innovators do their best work in life at an older age. They accomplish their genius through trial and error. Examples of these innovators are Steve Jobs, Mark Twain, and Alfred Hitchcock.

Older people may give a bunch of reasons for saying they are too old to start a business, but they are just excuses, many of which are defended with misinformation. Now we have plenty of data and reasons to support why being in your later years is an asset, not a liability when starting a business. If you are in your early thirties, forties, or older, it is not too late to start a business. Don't let your age deter you from pursuing your dream. Ultimately, a solid business idea paired with flawless execution, not a fresh face, is what leads to success in business.

CONCLUSION

WHY PERSONAL DEVELOPMENT....

We never stop growing. Of course, between the ages of 18 and 25 we stop physically growing, but our mind never stops growing. So we have two options: mold it, or ignore it. Entrepreneurs are the types of people who push boundaries, and in pushing boundaries, they push themselves. That means, they mold their ever-growing sense of self to become better and better. They push boundaries in themselves and the world around them. And that's essential. For an entrepreneur to stop growing, they grind to a halt, become disillusioned, and businesses become unsuccessful.

NEVER STOP LEARNING

Education is key. We are always learning from the world around us, striving to better understand how things work. Entrepreneurs need to maintain levels of education, otherwise, life can start to become quite frustrating. From computing courses to an ACBSP online MBA, there are always routes available to further an understanding of the industry. Every new thing learned can become assimilated into the way the company is run, pushing it to higher and higher levels. The ongoing personal education of the CEO is essential for humility and progress, and should never be overlooked.

BUILD OTHERS UP

When you're growing on a personal level, you're better able to understand how important that is to others. As an employer, you're duty-bound, at least by your sense of morality, to help your employees find fulfillment in their role. As you build yourself personally, it's easier to understand and be sympathetic to how others want to grow, but it's also far easier to offer them advice that is relevant to their desires. Not only does this make you a great boss, but it also helps you to encourage your workforce to go from strength to strength, making them far more efficient, loyal, and effective.

ENJOY NON-WORK RELATED ACTIVITIES

Many entrepreneurs are true workaholics, some putting in well over 10 hours a day. While this might be necessary on occasion, it certainly isn't good for anyone in the long run. Putting time into extra-curricular hobbies can help you to unwind, making it far easier to focus on days at work. But it can also help you to grow as a person outside of work, keep you fit, hone your hand-eye coordination, and practice your social skills – all of which are useful once you get back into the boardroom.

PUSH YOURSELF

To feel pride in ourselves, we need to achieve. Personal development is about pushing ourselves to try new things, overcome boundaries, and further our understanding. Personal development is about always achieving the next level of excellence, and being proud of what we can do. Every time we learn a new skill, we have added an extra string to our bow. This makes us happier in ourselves, but also more successful in business. As humans, we like to overcome adversity, and it's important to push ourselves through difficult times and academic struggles to grow and develop on a personal level.

Personal development is important for everyone, but especially for entrepreneurs. It helps to keep you grounded, be a better employer, but most of all, it makes you continually improve in business.